The Inequality of Nations

THE

INEQUALITY

OF

NATIONS

ROBERT W. TUCKER

Basic Books, Inc., Publishers

NEW YORK

Library of Congress Cataloging in Publication Data

Tucker, Robert W
  The inequality of nations.

  Includes bibliographical references and index.
  1. Equality of states.   2.   Self-defense (International law)   I.   Title.
JX4003.T82   341.26   76-9673
ISBN: 0–465–03245–1

For Joan, Peter, Bobby

Contents

Preface

THE CHALLENGE to international inequality, we are insistently warned, is the great issue of our time. It will dominate the future of world politics and increasingly displace the traditional conflicts of the past. In doing so, it will transform the character of state relations. The transformation is presumably already well underway.

This essay is an inquiry into the nature and meaning of the challenge to global inequality. I have been prompted to write it largely out of protest against the intellectual confusion that has attended current discussions of equality in relation to international society. In part, this confusion is simply an extension of the confusion that continues to attend discussions of equality in relation to domestic society. In part, however, it is also due to the failure to distinguish properly between domestic society and the greater society beyond. It makes a great deal of difference whether the subjects of equality are individuals or collectives (states). Similarly, it makes a great deal of difference whether the issues equality must raise are considered from the vantage point of a society that has set reasonably well-defined and effective limits to social conflicts or one that has not. These admonitions would seem almost self-evident. Yet the failure to observe them remains commonplace, as the following pages illustrate.

The substance of this study was initially presented in a series of seminars at The Lehrman Institute during 1974–75. A portion of it appeared as two articles in *Commentary* magazine under the titles "A New International Order?" (February 1975) and "Egalitarianism and International Politics" (September 1975).

I am indebted to many friends and colleagues for their help in writing this book. The members of the Lehrman Institute seminars provided sharp, but much needed, criticism. My colleagues at The Washington Center of Foreign Policy Research have contributed indirectly to this volume, as they have to earlier writings, by virtue of the continuing exchange of ideas on international politics. I am particularly grateful, however, to Pavel Machala, Piero Gleijeses, and Roger Hansen. Each played an important role in the development of the ideas contained in this study. Each read the manuscript at various stages and gave valuable suggestions. This is all the more remarkable since each maintained throughout serious points of disagreement with my outlook and analysis. The most persistent critic, Pavel Machala, kept my interest in the work alive through his constant questions; I am all the more obligated to him for this.

A final note of thanks must go to Catherine Grover who has taken care of this manuscript with her usual quiet efficiency.

I

Introduction: The Traditional System

THE HISTORY of the international system is a history of inequality par excellence. This is so not simply because political collectives vary greatly in those natural endowments that contribute to their power and wealth but also because of the basic condition in which they have always existed. It is understandable that the natural inequalities of states should impress the observer of state relations. In their physical extent, population, natural resources, and geographic position, states are, as it were, born unequal; so much so, indeed, that by comparison the natural inequalities among individuals appear almost marginal. Moreover, to the inequalities that attend the birth of political collectives must be added the unevenness that marks their subsequent development. The age of industrial civilization has strikingly accentuated this unevenness of development, thereby heightening earlier disparities of power and wealth.

Even so, what has made the international system a system of inequality par excellence are not merely these disparities—however important they may be—but the condition in which its members have existed in the past and from which they have yet to emerge. It is the condition of a society marked by the absence of effective collective procedures, competitive rather than cooperative, and lacking in commitment to a common good that has insured that differences in power and wealth will be employed to perpetuate inequality. The international system, Raymond Aron has observed, "has always been anarchical and oligarchical: anarchical because of the absence of a monopoly of legitimate violence, oligarchical (or hierarchic) in that, without civil society, rights depend largely on might." * This formulation may be varied slightly to underscore the point at hand by saying that the international system has always been in essence oligarchical (unequal) largely because it has been anarchical.

The international anarchy has not been devoid of institutional forms. Clearly, these forms are not the forms of civil society. Whether they may nevertheless be considered as constitutive of order depends upon whether the prevailing principle of self-help that characterizes them is considered compatible with order. Self-help, as the very term suggests, is the "right" of the state to determine when its legitimate interests are threatened, or violated, and to employ such coercive measures as it may deem necessary to vindicate those interests.† Viewed in the abstract, this institution points to the equality of states, for the right of self-help is equally available to all. In international law, the right of self-help that all states are held to possess as a consequence of their sovereignty and independence is presumably one of the distinguishing features, if not *the* distinguishing feature, of their legal equality. In practice, it has always been a prime expression of the essential inequality of states, since the utility of a right of self-help is of necessity dependent upon the power at the disposal of those exercising this right. Among unequals, in the absence of other and moderating factors, a right of self-help at best may be expected to preserve existing inequalities. More likely, it will function, as self-help has all too often functioned in the past, to increase inequalities between the strong and the weak. What Thucydides records the Athenians as saying to the Melians—that the powerful exact what they can, and the weak grant what they must—is true of any state

---

* Raymond Aron, *Progress and Disillusion: The Dialectics of Modern Society* (New York: Praeger, 1968), p. 160. Of course, oligarchy exists within civil society as well. That "rights depend largely on might" is a necessary, though not a sufficient, condition for oligarchy in international society. It is the "natural" inequalities of collectives and their unevenness of development that, along with their anarchical situation, guarantees oligarchy.

† In effect, self-help also encompasses the "right" to define one's legitimate interests. At any rate, this has largely been true in the case of the powerful.

system that is governed by only the unimpeded "right" of self-help.*

It is these considerations that have led some to conclude that self-help is subject to no constraints other than power itself, that it is a power not a right, and that the international system is characterized by the absence of right and order. Even those who have dissented from this view—asserting, instead, that self-help is a right, not merely a power—have had to concede that an order based on self-help has singular defects that make it only minimally satisfactory. Where the determination and vindication of rights is left to the interested parties, uncertainty must prevail. Moreover, where self-help is the principal institutional expression of order for a society whose members are vastly unequal in power, the tendency must arise to throw the mantle of right over those uses of power that, whatever their proper characterization, prove effective.

In principle, the differences between the above responses to self-help are clear enough. In practice, however, these differences may be quite marginal. How marginal they will be is not a question that can be answered in the abstract but will depend upon the constraints on behavior operative in a given period and on the extent to which such constraints permit a meaningful distinction to be drawn between self-help as a right rather than as a mere power.

The extreme consequences of self-help were at least partially avoided in the traditional state system by virtue of other and mod-

---

* This is not to say that the inequalities to which a system of self-help may give rise are necessarily greater than the inequalities found within civil society. Indeed, it is civil society that is necessarily a source of inequality, whereas it is at least possible to imagine a system of self-help that maintains a condition of rough equality among its members. By concentrating power in the hands of a few, the state is invariably a source of at least one form of inequality. A "state" in which coercive power is shared equally by all, and in which all are equally competent to determine the circumstances in which coercion is employed, would be a contradiction in terms. But if the state is a fundamental source of inequality, it is also the source of an equality that is not subject to the uncertainties and vicissitudes that must attend the pursuit of equality in a system governed by self-help. For the equality the latter may give rise to rests, at bottom, on the continued ability of each to vindicate its claims to equality. The equality that characterizes a system of self-help is, at best, precarious.

erating factors, particularly the balance of power. To be sure, the balance of power itself formed the principal political expression of self-help. At the same time, there is no gainsaying the contention that the balance operated on the whole to moderate the mutual behavior of the great powers. Nor does it seriously detract from this assessment to point out that war has been the indispensable, if ultimate, means to the effective functioning of the balance of power. In the past, at any rate, the principal promise of the balance was not the avoidance of war but the prevention of hegemony by any single great power over the others. It is only an age that has come to fear the dangers of war between the great powers almost as much as the dangers of hegemony that can no longer accept what an earlier age took for granted. The avoidance of war between the great powers is no longer merely a hoped-for outcome; in what is now termed a balance of deterrent power, belief in this outcome has become a psychological and moral necessity for the continued and effective support of the new balance.

Of relevance here is the issue of whether the balance operated historically to protect the interests of the weak. (We do not raise the further issue of whether the balance operated to reduce inequalities between the strong and the weak. There is no evidence that it ever had—or, for that matter, was ever designed to have—this effect. Nor has the claim that it has had this effect ever been seriously put forth on behalf of the balance.) The judgment that the balance "not only guaranteed the existence of small states, but assured them of a certain autonomy, a power of independent action," * is, its historical merits apart, not one that follows from the inherent logic of the system. Logically, there is no more reason why the balance should not eventuate in the domination of the weak than in their independence. To the extent that the balance of power was understood to mean the even distribution of power, that distribution implied, above all, a rough equality of the powerful. It is, after all, no accident that until

---

* Herbert Butterfield, "The Balance of Power," in *Diplomatic Investigations: Essays in the Theory of International Politics,* Herbert Butterfield and Martin Wight, eds. (Cambridge: Harvard Univ. Press, 1966), p. 142.

very recently claims to equality regularly originated from the strong rather than from the weak and that these claims were typically made in the spirit, if not the name, of the balance. That the weak might also benefit from the rough equality of the strong was an incidental result not intrinsic to the operation of the balance.

If the balance of power often functioned to preserve the independence of small states, it also operated to sacrifice the interests of the weak. Although the justification of the balance ultimately lay in its promise to bring both order and security to the states—all states—comprising international society, the price of order might nevertheless require the sacrifice of a particular state's security and, in the extreme, perhaps even its independence. Obscured by doctrine, this paradox has always inhered in the operation of the balance of power. Hence the occasions during preceding centuries in which the great powers equated order with their equality and the latter with their equal aggrandizement. Albert Sorel has given the classic description of how the operation of the balance of power led, in eighteenth-century Europe, to the system of great power partitions that "confused the equity of the deed with the equality of the shares, the justice of the operation with the niceness of the balance. . . ." * In the nineteenth century, the principle of equal aggrandizement, often termed the principle of compensation, was increasingly satisfied through the acquisition of territory and people beyond Europe. Indeed, it is only in retrospect that we can fully appreciate the extent to which such moderation as the balance of power introduced in Europe depended upon the immoderation of its working in the world outside Europe. It is in the closing period of the traditional system, roughly in the three decades preceding World War I, that a structure of imposed inequality between the core of European states and the Asian and African periphery of colonies, protectorates, and semi-sovereign entities became the most pronounced.†

* Albert Sorel, *Europe and the French Revolution: The Political Traditions of the Old Regime,* trans. and ed. by Alfred Cobban and J. W. Hunt (London: Collins, 1969), p. 67.

† Even within Europe, the moderation introduced by the balance is easily exaggerated. The argument is often made that by the nineteenth century, and certainly by the

What the balance of power could not lay claim to, international law could scarcely achieve. It may be true, as Marx insisted, that all law is a "law of inequality." But some law is still more unequal than others. The traditional system of international law affords a striking example of the law of the strong. To be sure, among the fundamental rights of states in international law there has always been the right of equality. As an attribute of statehood, that right could have little, if any, meaning for peoples who, until the present century, were not admitted to the select circle of sovereign states. Thus for centuries the equality principle in international law coexisted with the colonial system, the latter being no less sanctioned in law than the claim to equality. And if the equality principle has been employed in this century on behalf of the self-determination of formerly subject and dependent peoples, it has not been so employed as a legal principle but as a principle of justice invoked by the weak against the rights in law of the strong.

How was the colonial system in its successive phases reconciled with the equality principle? The formal answer is simply that this principle, as a principle of law, applied only to collectives possessing full international legal personality. Equality was an attribute of sovereign states. As such, equality was not denied by virtue of the fact that many peoples were not accorded this status. If they were not accorded this status, it was presumably because they failed to meet

---

close of that century, the legitimacy of the various states of Europe, however small and weak, stood as an effective restriction on the license with which the great might employ their power. In Europe, at any rate, the destruction of an independent sovereignty was no longer accepted. But this "right to existence" of the small and weak was never as secure as retrospective reflection suggests. Certainly it was not something that was immanent in the very development of the international system. It might always be jeopardized once the conditions productive of moderation began to break down. The occasion in which they were most likely to do so was, of course, a European war involving the great powers. In a sense, then, war among the great powers formed the crucial test of the viability of any right to existence of the small. If in World War I the right survived the test, this was because those who challenged the balance of power were defeated. In retrospect, we know that had the challenge succeeded, the rights of a number of the small states, including even the right to existence, would have been jeopardized.

the standards required of sovereign states in international law. Initially identified with Christianity, by the nineteenth century liberal Civilization largely replaced Christianity as the source of the standards required for membership in the society of nations. These standards, as is well known, were those of European liberal civilization. Though not without a substantial measure of ambiguity, they were generally held to require not only an effective government over a defined territory but a willingness and ability to accept the obligations of European international law, particularly those obligations relating to protection of the life, liberty, and property of foreigners.

In all its variations, the justification given for the inequalities attending the relations between European and non-European peoples stemmed from the presumed inability of the latter to meet the standards of Civilization. Their exclusion from participation, or from full participation, in the society of nations was, for this reason, considered unavoidable. At the same time, their position of dependency upon the civilized nations was considered equally unavoidable if they were eventually to meet the standards of civilized states. Accordingly, the inequalities of the colonial structure were judged both inevitable and just—inevitable because reciprocity could not reasonably be expected from those lacking in civilization, just because the primacy of the European states served to confer upon the backward the benefits of civilization. John Stuart Mill only expressed the prevailing nineteenth-century outlook, liberal and otherwise, when he wrote: "To suppose that the same international customs, and the same rule of international morality, can obtain between one civilised nation and another, and between civilised nations and barbarians, is a grave error, and one which no statesman can fall into. . . . Among many reasons why the same rules cannot be applicable to situations so different, the two following are among the most important. In the first place, the rules of ordinary international morality imply reciprocity. But barbarians will not reciprocate. . . . In the next place, nations which are still barbarous have not got beyond the period during which it is likely to be for their benefit that they should be

9

conquered and held in subjection by foreigners." * Marx was even more explicit on the benefits the advanced countries would confer on "backward" peoples. His attitude toward European colonial expansion was one of support of the results this expansion would ultimately bring to stagnant societies. With respect to British rule in India Marx wrote: "England has to fulfill a double mission in India: one destructive, the other regenerating—the annihilation of old Asiatic society, and the laying of the material foundation of Western society in Asia." †

Until our own time, then, the principle of equality in international law could have little, if any, relevance for those peoples, who comprise a majority of humanity, considered either outside or on the periphery of the society of states. Within this society, did it serve to protect the interests of the weak? In part, the answer must be found in the relationship between international law and the balance of power. To the extent that international law depended for its effectiveness upon the maintenance of a balance of power, and that dependence was critical, this legal system had somehow to accommodate itself to the employment of methods that not only escaped legal control but also seemed to deny the very possibility of a legal ordering of state relations. War—preventive war included—was an essential means to the maintenance of the balance of power. Given the dependence of international law on the balance, war was an indispensable prerequisite for the realization of an effective legal order. At the same time, war undertaken for the maintenance of the balance was an insurmountable obstacle to the realization of an effective—even a minimal—legal order. Hence the apparent anomaly of a legal system that did not, and seemingly could not, consistently draw the most elementary distinction any system of law must make;

---

* John Stuart Mill, "A Few Words on Non-Intervention," *Dissertations and Discussions: Political, Philosophical, and Historical* (Boston: William Spencer, 1864–67), vol. 3, pp. 251–52.

† Karl Marx, "The Future Results of British Rule in India," in Shlomo Avineri, *Karl Marx on Colonialism and Modernization* (New York: Doubleday, 1969), pp. 132–33.

Introduction: The Traditional System

the distinction between the lawful and the unlawful use of force.*

The customary liberty accorded states to resort to war in order to maintain the balance of power formed only the most notorious justification of their primordial right of self-help. In fact, it was scarcely necessary to place this liberty in a separate category, since it was readily encompassed by the more general "right" of self-preservation that states took for granted.† Traditionally claimed not only to protect the state's physical person but also those interests that collectively comprise the state's security, and consequently its "existence" in the broader sense of political independence, the right of self-preservation affords the classic example of the license to which the institution of self-help may lead. This license was not materially diminished by insisting that a right of self-preservation must be interpreted to mean a right of self-defense, since in the latter case virtually the same latitude prevailed both with respect to the scope of interests comprising security and independence and with respect to the acts in response to which a state might resort to forcible measures.

The inability of international law to set meaningful limits to the state's right of self-help explains the distinctive manner in which forcible change in the status quo has been dealt with in law. Provided that the change was effective, it has regularly been considered constitutive of a new status quo endowed with the same legitimacy as the status quo it replaced. That the new status quo originated in a violation of the rights of other states has not been considered decisive in determining its legitimacy. Once the change, whatever its origins,

---

* According to the legal doctrine prevailing until World War I, the act of resorting to war was neither legal nor illegal, but "extralegal" in the sense of an event occurring in nature. However fictitious this doctrine, it nevertheless accurately reflected the dilemma of an order dependent for its effectiveness upon the maintenance of a balance of power, and consequently upon methods that remained impervious to effective legal control. To the extent this dilemma—indeed, contradiction—was resolved, it was not on the level of law. Instead, one must look to the various inhibitions—material and moral—that operated to restrain balance-of-power policies in preceding centuries.

† "In the last resort," declared the greatest of English writers on international law of the nineteenth century, "almost the whole of the duties of states are subordinated to the right of self-preservation" (W. E. Hall, *International Law,* 8th ed. [Oxford: Clarendon Press, 1924], p. 322).

was no longer effectively contested by the interested parties, it has been deemed to create a new status quo, both in fact and in law. Territorial change brought about by force, peace treaties imposed upon the defeated, and, in general, treaties reflecting an extreme relationship of duress and inequality have all been regularly sanctioned in international law. It was, of course, the absence of effective collective procedures, or the pervasiveness of the institution of self-help, that must account for the virtually unrestricted operation of the principle *ex injuria jus oritur,* and thus for the near equation of law with power.

Given these characteristics of traditional international law, it is not surprising that many have seen it as the negation of law and not merely as the operation of an admittedly defective legal order, though a legal order nonetheless. Certainly the defects of that system were little short of monumental. The prevalence of self-help ensured that when a serious conflict of interest arose, it would be settled on the basis of the relative power of the disputants. It was not simply the general affinity of right and power, then, that set international law apart, for this affinity has been characteristic of most legal systems history has known. What set international law apart, and pointed, as did nothing else, to its tenuous claim as law, was its inability to distinguish right (and law) from a *particular* exercise of power, provided only that the exercise proved effective. Yet in the absence of the institutions characteristic of domestic society, the only alternatives to validating the effects of the unlawful use of power have been either to challenge power directly with power or to refuse to recognize the legality of a situation brought about by unlawful power. The former alternative necessarily carried with it the prospect of war. The latter alternative, if considered as an alternative to war, could result either in demonstrating the impotence of the law or in placing those situations originating in unlawful behavior outside the pale of international law. Not only would these results fail to undo the effects of unlawful power; they could merely serve to weaken further whatever standing international law might have.

In effect, then, war—or the meaningful threat of war—has been the only reliable response to undoing the unlawful effects of power, above all in the case of strong states. In the absence of that response, international law could adjust to the new situation, however unlawful its origins, only by recognizing its validity. To the jurist bearing the perspective of municipal law, the adjustment might seem the denial of the minimal requirements of law. From a different and broader perspective, however, the adjustment simply reflected the price to be paid for securing at least a modicum of order in state relations.

The significance of the equality principle followed largely from the characteristics of the traditional system sketched above. The equality of states expressed, first and foremost, an equal right or freedom to determine the circumstances in which the state's legitimate interests were threatened and to take the measures necessary to protect those interests. The equality of states thus consisted primarily of the recognition by others of an equal claim to the right of self-help and, above all, the right to wage war. And since this right has always been the hallmark of a state's independence, it has never been easy to distinguish between the equality and the independence of states. States were equal insofar as they were independent. In turn, they were independent insofar as they enjoyed the right of self-help. The conventional definition of independence—the absence of a legal relation of superiority and subordination—is but another way of making the same point.

It will be apparent that if the equality of states consists esentially of the equal claim to the right of self-help, the vindication in practice of equality must depend upon the relative power of states. Consequently, the freedom of action traditionally claimed by states in the name of equality—or independence—jeopardized even the elementary equality of civil society: equal protection of the law. It did so for the reason that in a system governed by self-help, rights will tend to be coextensive with power. Equality before the law necessarily assumes that when a dispute arises between states, disparities of power will not affect the determination of their respective rights and duties. Without this assumption, there is no way in which the parties in dispute may be treated juridically as equals. But self-help excludes, almost by definition, this assumption, since disparities of power are of its very essence. In consequence, there is an inherent antinomy between the principle of equality before the law and the principle of self-help.*

Against this pattern of inequality the economic relations of states shared much the same characteristics as their political-legal relations. This was evidently the case for mercantilism, which equated economic relations with relations of state power. Mercantilism was, and openly professed to be, the economic version of political self-help. Inequality was its essence. Liberalism, on the other hand, not only sought to separate economic from political relations but to represent itself as the very antithesis of the inequality that characterized mercantilism. Whereas mercantilism equated self-help with the state and with collective inequality, liberalism equated self-help with the individual and with individual equality of opportunity. Liberalism could do so because it assumed, among other things, that economic self-help would be divorced from the political (power) and that in consequence the economic units (individuals) would deal with each other from the position of an equality of power.

The mercantilist system of inequality encompassed both those collectives at a similar level of socio-economic development as well as

* Although international jurists have not been oblivious to the obstacles self-help poses to any form of legal equality, they have, perhaps understandably, shied away from drawing the evident implications. In the classic treatise on equality in international law, self-help is seen as an "important limitation upon equality of legal capacity." (E. D. Dickinson, *The Equality of States in International Law* [Cambridge: Harvard Univ. Press, 1920], p. 274). But whereas equality of legal capacity is not considered indispensable to a system of law, equal protection of the law is commonly so regarded. It is for this reason that even the more skeptical of international jurists hesitated to draw the full consequences of self-help. They continue to do so. Thus Julius Stone, in defending the principle of equality in international society against the charge that it is a myth, declares: "In terms . . . of the doctrine's reference to mere equality before the law, that is, the title of all states to assert before international law such benefits as that law confers, the cry of 'myth' cannot literally stand" ("Approaches to the Notion of International Justice," in *The Future of the International Legal Order, vol. 1: Trends and Patterns,* Richard A. Falk and Cyril E. Black, eds. [Princeton: Princeton Univ. Press, 1969], p. 424). Yet Stone goes on to note: "The deeper meaning of the cry of myth lies in the fact . . . that not merely the legal status of particular states, but their very existence and whole subsequent life, are usually the product of inequalities of power rather than of impartial principles of justice." The existence of states, however, is not endangered by power inequalities per se as much as by the self-help attending those inequalities.

collectives at disparate levels of development. It was designed to preserve and increase inequality within the core of European states and between this core and the non-European periphery. The liberal system promised in theory to apply universally. In practice, however, its assumptions extended only to those peoples at approximately the same level of development, that is, the peoples sharing Western civilization. Between them and the backward peoples liberalism's original promise was displaced by manifest relations of inequality. If even here the inequality of liberal colonialism seemed less obtrusive than its mercantilist predecessor, it was largely because the coercive element in economic relations was normally less overt than in political relations. In fact, inequalities of economic power worked roughly according to the same logic as inequalities of political power. The view that with respect to backward regions economic inequalities would not have consequences comparable to political inequalities proved illusory. What was instead demonstrated was that among unequals in social-economic development an unimpeded right to trade—and to invest capital—would have comparable effects to the unimpeded right to self-help among collectives of unequal natural endowments. Rather than to reduce existing inequalities of wealth, these effects would operate, as indeed they did, to increase inequalities between the backward and developed regions.

It is in the light of these considerations that the traditional international system must be judged a system of inequality par excellence. If there is a limited truth in the contention that the institutions of international society—the balance of power, international law, diplomatic practice—served to moderate the extreme consequences of self-help, and thereby to provide a semblance of order, the larger truth is that these institutions functioned on balance to legitimize power and the inequalities power created or sustained. Perhaps nothing better illustrates the essential inegalitarianism of international society than the fact, already noted, that until very recent times the significant claims to equality have invariably been claims advanced by the strong against the strong. The only equality this society has known has been a rough and precarious equality of the strong.

II

A New International System?

I

TRADITIONAL PATTERNS of inequality in international society are widely challenged today. Differences may and do persist over the lengths to which this challenge can be expected to go in the years ahead and the consequences it will have if permitted to run its logical course. These differences do not affect the view that for the present, at any rate, we are in a period when inequalities once accepted as part of the natural order of things are no longer so accepted. Nor do they affect the judgment that many of the inequalities endemic to international society in the past are no longer sustainable.

This is all too clearly the case with respect to formal inequalities. Although inequalities of status have not altogether disappeared, they remain as no more than vestiges of an order that has today lost almost any semblance of legitimacy. Even if it is argued that in a number of respects a *de facto* colonialism persists, the point remains—and it is an all important one—that as a *de jure* institution colonialism has passed into history. The same must be said of the varieties of formalized relationships—special regimes, capitulations, extraterritoriality—that once expressed the supremacy of the West over the "backward" peoples and territories of the world. Thus the "unequal treaty," though in concept not free from either ambiguity or abuse, is everywhere condemned. That condemnation reflects the broad consensus that has come to view almost any formal inequality with disfavor. Despite the continued strictures of many international jurists that legal equality is not to be identified with an equal capacity for rights, the thrust of contemporary international law has plainly been in the direction of the negation of status.

The rapid erosion, if not the complete disappearance, of formal inequalities once sanctioned by law is, in turn, commonly considered to reflect an emergent political equality that cannot be adequately assessed simply by the voting procedures of international organization. Even within the state, the measure of political equality is not exhausted by the yardstick of "one man, one vote." Its degree of achievement must also be judged by existing inequalities of wealth and power and the extent to which these inequalities actually determine and perpetuate a given social order. In international society, a roughly similar reasoning presumably may be applied. The measure of political equality is not exhausted by the observance of the "one state, one vote" rule in international organizations and conferences. One must also ask to what degree disparities in wealth and power determine relations between the strong and the weak. Here, as elsewhere, political equality, the argument runs, is a function of the totality of restraints, formal and informal, placed on the use of power. To the extent that military and, to an increasing degree, even economic power can no longer operate in the manner of the past, the prospect materializes not only for a substantially greater measure of political equality but, ultimately, for the emergence of a greater measure of economic equality.

It is in this manner that international society is increasingly perceived as following a course of development roughly parallel to that already traced by Western societies. In the extension of statehood to peoples formerly held outside the system, in the steady abandonment of formal inequalities of status among those comprising the system, and in the growing restraints placed on the use of power, the international society of today is seen as scarcely resembling the international society of the pre-World War I period. So, too, the legal order of this society is seen as scarcely resembling traditional international law. A new egalitarianism has arisen in which an emergent political equality has been attended not only by the demand for equality of opportunity but also by the demand for a greater measure of equality of condition.

II

The contemporary challenge to inequality has been almost as sudden as it has been pervasive. Of course, we may find harbingers of the opposition to inequality we experience today not only in the interwar period but in the years preceding World War I. The egalitarianism of nation-states that is a commonplace today was not unknown at the turn of the century. Nor was the logic of this new egalitarianism obscured to its adherents. The equation of the state and the nation not only invested the state with a legitimacy it had not previously possessed; that equation also gave to the claim of state equality an appeal and force it had never before enjoyed. For the equality of nation-states evoked, if nothing else, a far more persuasive analogy with the ideal of individual equality than had the analogy earlier drawn between states and men. The ideal of the nation carried with it a quality of "naturalness," hence a quality of individuality, that could be attributed to the state alone only with considerable difficulty. Once the implications of this ideal were accepted, it followed that nation-states need be no more identical than men to claim that they had an equal value by virtue of their individuality. And in the case of nations, as in the case of individuals, it was argued that equality was violated when individuality was suppressed, through denial of political independence, or when it was robbed of self-respect by the disabilities—political, legal, and economic—that effectively deprive a collective of full participation in international society.

But if the new egalitarianism of nations was eventually to serve both as a prime factor in the creation of new states and as a powerful rallying cry for the removal of inequalities held to deprive peoples of self-respect, these were consequences that largely materialized only in the years following World War II. They are indeed the consequences that form part of the basis for the present challenge to inequality. Prior to World War I, however, they appeared as little more than the first winds that herald the possibility of a coming storm. At the time of the outbreak of hostilities in 1914, the inequalities—formal and substantive—that characterized the international system were certainly no less than the inequalities of a century earlier; in many respects, they were considerably greater. Between the advanced societies of the West and the peoples of Asia and Africa, disparities of wealth and power had dramatically increased. In turn, these disparities had eventuated in a system of imposed inequalities that was more marked and pervasive than ever before.

The war dealt a severe blow to the traditional system. Not only did it weaken those who had been the principal custodians of the system; it partially discredited them as well. The successful maintenance of this system had depended upon its moderation, not so much with respect to the small and weak states—let alone to the subject peoples—but with respect to the mutual behavior of the great. The immoderation shown by the great powers toward one another revealed the vulnerability of the traditional system and, by so doing, opened the issue of its legitimacy. To critics from within, the war made clear the need to find a substitute for the methods that had led the trustees of civilization to such carnage. The Wilsonian alternative was one of reform. Through the observance of new restraints, a chastened yet ultimately reinvigorated concert of powers, now led by America, would maintain a world not markedly different in its political and social structure from the pre-1914 world. Self-determination, though in principle of universal applicability, was given immediate relevance only in Europe. Elsewhere, it was to be realized gradually through legal, that is, peaceful, methods and then only once the colonial peoples had accepted liberal values and had been adequately schooled in the methods of self government.*

---

* Even the Wilsonian view implied that self-determination in Asia and Africa was scarcely more than an abstract ideal. This view was reflected in the Covenant of the League of Nations. The guiding principle behind the League's mandate system was

A New International System?

Wilson's anti-imperialism was as much apologetic as it was reformist. Even so, it was not without effect in many of the colonial countries where the promise of self-determination was given a more literal interpretation than Wilson and others had intended. The expectations of subject peoples had already been aroused by the propaganda tactics the belligerents employed against one another in the course of the war. Not for the first time in their history, the European powers, pursuing their respective reasons of state, saw fit to undermine the authority by which each ruled. Although this common effort in subversion was short-lived, it made a considerable impression on subject peoples.*

Of still greater importance, however, was the effect on emerging nationalist leadership in the colonial world of the Russian Revolution and the Bolsheviks' subsequent denunciation of colonialism. Whereas Wilson had aroused the desire for the self-determination of subject peoples in large measure unintentionally, Lenin did so deliberately in the hope that a rising wave of anti-colonialism would bring with it Communist world revolution. And if the hope proved abortive, there is no question of the considerable impact the Russian Revolution had in the colonial world and the influence the Soviet Union

---

not the promotion of self-determination but the orderly division of the defeated state's colonial possessions among the victors. Nor could self-determination be seriously considered a goal of either British or French administrators of empire during the interwar period. Natives in British colonies were deemed to possess none of the necessary cultural or social prerequisites for self-government. Nor was it considered at all probable that they could acquire such requisites in the foreseeable future. British "trusteeship" during the interwar period was scarcely distinguishable in content from the forms of administration that prevailed before World War I. According to the policy of assimilation pursued in the French colonies, self-determination could at best be interpreted as applying to the individual, operating within the context of *"la plus grande France,"* not to the collectivity. Whereas for Britain self-determination of the colonies was at least admitted in principle, though excluded in practice, for France it was excluded as a matter of principle.

* "It did not occur to the Allied governments that the propaganda they employed against the Central Empires would affect their own empires fundamentally, or that by proclaiming the principle of self-determination they had laid the axe at the roots of their own colonial domains. But after 1918 they could only keep other nations in political subjection at the cost of moral inconsistency, except in so far as it could be maintained that they were unfit for self-government" (Alfred Cobban, *National Self-Determination* [Chicago: Univ. of Chicago Press, 1944], p. 124).

would continue to have in the interwar period by virtue of its support—however selective—of anti-colonial activities.

The dependent peoples were not only made the objects of war-aims propaganda, and later of revolutionary propaganda; they were also made participants in the conflict. Britain and France drew upon their colonial populations to replenish their armed forces; they also became more dependent on their colonies for food and raw materials than they had previously been. In these and still other ways, the colonial countries were drawn into the great conflict. Their participation, however, was not without a price. The precedent of Asian and African soldiers in Europe fighting with white men against white men could not be a comforting one for the colonial powers. Nor could the latter escape the consequences of an acknowledged dependence on the subject peoples. Among the then-emerging nationalist movements, an awareness of the role played by the colonies in the war stimulated demands—as in India—for self-government.

Despite these effects, a comparison of the pre-1914 system with the system that emerged from the war shows more continuity than change. It does so despite the League of Nations and the change that was occurring—at least, among the Western democracies—in men's attitude toward war and conquest. It is quite true that after World War I the once commonly accepted view that war represented an instrument of progress, particularly when employed to spread the civilization of superior peoples, ceased to be fashionable or even acceptable. When Mussolini declared in the course of the Italian conquest of Ethiopia that "Fascism sees in the imperialistic spirit a manifestation of its vitality," he expressed a view which would have been found quite commonplace at the turn of the century. By the 1930s, however, it was widely considered not only as unacceptable but as curiously archaic. The Western colonial powers might, and did, justify their holding on to what they had gotten through the "imperialistic spirit" of a generation or two earlier; they would no longer condone the forcible acquisition of empire by others.

These considerations apart, the point remains that on balance, the interwar period conformed to traditional patterns of inequality.* Although the legitimacy of the more extreme manifestations of self-help—above all, armed force—was no longer accepted with the equanimity characteristic of an earlier era, the historic functions of military power remained largely unchanged. The current view taken of the "disutility" of military power was clearly not the view taken in the interwar period.

The measure of the transformation that has since occurred in this all-important aspect of state relations is apparent when we recall the expectations of the role played by military power that were entertained scarcely more than three decades ago. In the 1930s, the fear of expansion was a fear that still largely equated expansion with territorial conquest, or the functional equivalent thereof, and not with the precarious forms of influence we have since become accustomed to. Moreover, given the persisting expectation that pacification consequent upon military conquest would not prove too difficult, it followed that territorial expansion continued to confer the advantages such expansion had conferred in the past. In almost all the strategic calculations made by analysts on the eve of the Second World War, it was simply assumed that traditional methods of expansion remained essentially unchanged, as did the effects of such expansion on the balance of power.

Nor was it only with respect to the use made and expected of military power that the world of the 1930s was still very much a traditional world. It is instructive to remind ourselves that demands for equality in the interwar years were, in the main, the demands of states now, as indeed then, comprising the powerful and wealthy of international society. What was then popularly termed the struggle between the "haves" and the "have-nots" was in reality a struggle among the haves. In this respect as well, the interwar period clearly

* The conclusion of one of the more acute observers of this period may be allowed to stand. "The constant intrusion, or potential intrusion, of power renders almost meaningless any conception of equality between members of the international community" (E. H. Carr, *The Twenty Year's Crisis* [London: Macmillan & Co. Ltd., 1939], p. 166).

followed a traditional pattern. A majority of the have-nots of today had yet to achieve independence. With rare exception, they were not in a position to press for equalities that, for better or worse, are achievable only through the institution of the state. Among the have-nots of today that did enjoy independence then, the claims to equality, when heard at all by the haves, seem altogether modest by comparison with the claims of the developing states today.* What is increasingly taken as a commonplace today, that the division between the rich and the poor nations poses a grave danger to peace and stability, was then no more than the musing of a few seers. The contemporary persuasion that this division is morally repugnant was the possession of perhaps an even more select group. The conviction that justice requires the rich nations to help all peoples obtain a "minimum subsistence" could scarcely be seriously entertained by nations that had yet to recognize the precept of minimum subsistence in their domestic lives.

In these respects, the equality of the interwar period was substantially the equality of the pre-World War I period; that is, a rough and precarious equality of the great powers. The hierarchical ordering of international society remained what it had always been. This is not to say that the relationships between imperial states and dependent peoples went unchanged; but the changes that did occur nevertheless left intact the system of Western domination in Asia and Africa. In retrospect, it is easy enough to trace the symptoms that were soon to prove fatal to this system. To those who find these symptoms primarily in the erosion of Western power and will, the years that followed World War I were, in the words of one observer, "paced by paper tigers. If the European empires did not display their weakness, that was because no one openly exposed it. Their equipment was indeed inspected, but the general belief was that these emperors still wore clothes." † To those who find these symptoms primarily in the capacity of Asians and Africans for self-renewal and for assimilation

* They consisted primarily of demands to abolish systems of unequal treaties imposed on them by the major powers.

† A. P. Thornton, *Doctrines of Imperialism* (New York: Wiley, 1965), p. 205.

of Western ideas, techniques, and institutions, the years that followed World War I demonstrated that the Western colonial powers faced a rising tide of revolt they could not possibly hope to stem.* Though they may differ over the relative significance of the various causes of decline and fall, a growing number of students of empire now conclude that the end was close at hand even before the coup de grace given by World War II.

At the time, however, the matter appeared otherwise, certainly to those "paper tigers" who, though placed on the defensive and obliged to justify their rule in terms of the benefits conferred upon the ruled, were nevertheless determined to hold on to empire for as long as possible. In a number of ways, World War I itself served to strengthen this determination. This was particularly so in the case of France, where a postwar sense of insecurity and weakness was partially compensated by the power and prestige felt to be conferred by empire. Elite and popular opinion alike not only emphasized—and exaggerated—the significance of the contribution made by the colonies to the war effort but subscribed to the view that France's security and her claims to great-power status were critically dependent upon the retention of her empire. *La plus grande France,* the "France of a hundred million," responded to the continued threat posed by Germany and to the emergence of the great continental states. Moreover, until well into the Second World War, the demands of the educated nationalist elite in the French colonies were for greater assimilation, not independence.

In Britain as well, the immediate aftermath of the war was marked by renewed determination to retain the empire, though this determination, in contrast to France, did not lay direct stress upon the empire as a vital ingredient of power and security. Rather, empire was a vital ingredient in British prestige, and therefore indirectly in British power and security. The empire had to be held because it represented a noble and sacred trust. Britain would lose her greatness if she were to abandon her responsibilities to peoples comprising almost a

* Geoffrey Barraclough, *An Introduction to Contemporary History* (London: C. A. Watts, 1964), pp. 153ff.

quarter of the world's population. Though now committed to the notion of trusteeship, with its promise that one day the dependent territories would assume responsibility for their own destiny, for as far as men cared to see the empire would remain intact. Trusteeship remained a concept implying primarily negative responsibilities; that is, the protection of the natives and the maintenance of law and order. A more positive definition, emphasizing development, was given only marginal consideration, since the colonial peoples were regarded as generations away from responsible government. "The hour when the native peoples would be fit for self-government," one writer has aptly observed, "lay so distant as to be as devoid of practical meaning as the Second Coming." *

It is true that this postwar reaction began to erode with the passing of time. In Britain, at any rate, the liberal and left intelligentsia showed itself increasingly hostile to imperial ideals and, eventually, to empire itself. Even in an earlier period, before World War I, liberal support for empire was seldom without qualification. The imperial commitment rested essentially on the belief "that political power tended constantly to deposit itself in a natural aristocracy, that power so deposited was morally valid, that it was not to be tamely surrendered before the claims of abstract democratic ideals, but was to be asserted and exercised with justice and mercy." † This conservative and inegalitarian belief could be reconciled with liberalism only if certain assumptions about the perfectability of man were credited. In order to justify present colonial rule, liberals, unlike the conservatives who held no illusions about the perfectability of man, had to believe that membership in the natural aristocracy could be

* Correlli Barnett, *The Collapse of British Power* (New York: Morrow, 1972), p. 289. Barnett finds the British Empire in the interwar period "one of the most outstanding examples of strategic over-extension in history," "a source of weakness and danger . . . rather than of strength" (p. 232). The French case is less clear, but there is no doubt that French expectations of what the empire might mean as a source of power and security were wildly exaggerated. Cf. Rudolf von Albertini, *Decolonization: The Administration and Future of the Colonies, 1919–1960* (New York: Doubleday, 1971), pp. 265–278.

† Eric Stokes, *The Political Ideas of English Imperialism* (Oxford: Oxford Univ. Press, 1960), pp. 10–11.

continually enlarged as a direct result of tutelary colonial rule. Only if it promoted this implicitly egalitarian ideal could liberals enthusiastically support empire. As the liberal-radicals discovered, once empire had been acquired, the fundamental question of whether acquisition was justified became irrelevant. Acquisition of empire was an irreversible act. Abandonment would not only be immoral, it would also inevitably lead to the absorption of the colonies by powers that were, on the one hand, Britain's competitors, and, on the other, less fit for governing. By the end of the nineteenth century the central issue for liberals was not whether empire was in Britain's best interest, but rather how best to administer the existing empire. Buttressed by the persuasion that imperialism was serving an indispensable tutelary mission, that it was an instrument for the realization of liberal-democratic ideals, and that its methods could be morally sustained, liberals' support for empire was assured.*

This persuasion was clearly shaken by World War I. It eroded throughout the interwar period, despite the momentary acceptance of empire on almost all sides in the years immediately following the war. For liberals broadly accepted the Wilsonian judgment—though it was not only Wilson's—that the war had been brought on largely by the imperialist policies of the great powers and the colonial rivalries thereby engendered. This being so, imperialism and its fruits became ever more suspect. Moreover, a deepening commitment to democracy and equality at home was bound to prove increasingly difficult to reconcile with the assertion of the right of one people to impose its rule on another, even when this rule was justified by the purpose of enabling subject peoples to rule themselves eventually.† Then, too, the acceptance of the tutelary mission was justified

---

* Bernard Porter has given a detailed analysis of the evolution of liberal, Fabian, and Labor attitudes toward empire before World War I (*Critics of Empire: British Radical Attitudes to Colonialism in Africa, 1895–1914* [New York: St. Martin's Press, 1968]).

† ". . . Imperialists reacted in four different ways to the apparent conflict between the ideals of Liberty and those of Empire. Either they reconciled their creed with Liberal beliefs, by regarding empire as a preparation for eventual independence, or at least as conveying a more real freedom and enlightenment; or they suppressed their scruples in deference to their view of what the national safety or greatness required;

not simply in terms of education for self-rule, or even for a certain kind of self-rule, but also in terms of the civilization that Europe brought to backward peoples. It was the belief in the intrinsic superiority of European civilization that from the start provided much of the self-assurance and élan of Western imperialism. In the interwar period, this self-assurance also began to erode in the solvent of an outlook that acknowledged the differences, though not the inequalities, of cultures. Among Western intelligentsia, the assertion of cultural superiority was henceforth considered the mark of the ignorant or, when employed to justify political expansion, the perverse.

These summary considerations point to some of the changes that were taking place in Western societies, changes that would have made it increasingly difficult in any event to hold on to empire in the long run. But the long run might have proved quite long indeed had it not been for World War II, the relative—though still strikingly precipitous—decline in power of the metropoles, and of course the telescoped developments occurring within the colonial countries. The fact is that up to the outbreak of war in 1939 the governments of the major colonial powers showed little disposition to accede to claims of independence made by nationalist movements in the dependent countries. Such concessions as were made to demands for self-government, particularly by the British, were viewed as mere changes in status within the empire, not as first steps toward dissociation from it. Moreover, prior to this time colonial emancipation movements tended to couch their demands in terms of greater participation in government, not in terms of outright independence. Nor is it at all clear that in the absence of the war, or of substantial outside assistance, these claims could have been vindicated before a substantial period. The most significant challenge to the British empire, the

---

or they decided that the principle of equality did not extend to 'inferior races' and tropic climates; or they largely abandoned the assumptions of liberalism and, with them, a sense of guilt. Imperialists of these two last categories were free to act as earlier Imperialists had done. . . . But in Great Britain these thorough-going Imperialists were never more than a minority in a nation which had traditionally considered itself the home of freedom . . ." (Richard Faber, *The Vision and the Need* [London: Faber and Faber, 1966], p. 130).

Indian Congress movement, demonstrated that if left to its own internal sources of strength it was still very far from possessing either the material power, popular support, or self-confidence to achieve its goals. In French territories, the demand was often one of increased integration and assimilation with the metropole. Thus in Algeria, native elites remained in favor of increased integration and assimilation until well into World War II. Elsewhere, the imbalance of power between the metropoles and indigenous challenges to their rule was still more striking. Given this imbalance, it is not surprising that the more acute critics of empire concluded that, in the words of one, the liquidation of empire might be a task of many decades.*

III

In considerable measure, the judgment made of the interwar period may also be made of the war years. Although the war was to bring momentous changes, these changes were scarcely foreshadowed either in the wartime declarations of the United Nations or in the institutions established to order the postwar world. Certainly, one may find repeated affirmation of the principle of the "sovereign equality" of all states. But the homage paid to this principle broke no new ground. Nor, for that matter, did the commitment to the self-determination of all peoples, in the absence of further specification by

* Thus the conclusion of M. J. Bonn (*The Crumbling of Empire* [London: G. Allen & Unwin, 1938], p. 423): ". . . the ultimate liquidation of domination . . . may be a task of decades or of centuries." In 1937 a report of the Royal Institute of International Affairs expressed the moderate view in declaring "that the road to independence will certainly be long" (*The Colonial Problem* [New York: Oxford Univ. Press, 1937], p. 232). Significantly, in his influential study, *The Twenty Years' Crisis,* E. H. Carr concluded a discussion on "the prospects of a new international order" by placing the struggle for equality at the center of efforts at reconstruction. "The inequality which threatened a world upheaval," Carr wrote, "was not inequality between individuals, nor inequality between classes, but inequality between nations" (p. 222). But the inequality he pointed to was the inequality of existing nations; that is, the inequality between the status quo and the revisionist powers in the interwar period. Carr had little to say about the challenge to inequality that would emerge from decolonization and that increasingly preoccupies us today.

those making the commitment, of the areas to which self-determination would be applied. Thus the pledge given in the Atlantic Charter (1941) to "respect the right of all peoples to choose the form of government under which they will live" was marked by extended speculation over whether it applied only to Europe or was also to be given at least selected application in the colonial world. It is clear that, in practice, the pledge was not intended to be given universal application, even by its American sponsors who professed to believe in the minimal equality of self-determination.

Clearer still is the absence of intent to go beyond a selective application of "minimal equality." The undertaking of the signatories of the Atlantic Charter "to further enjoyment by all states, great or small, victor or vanquished, of access, on equal terms, to the trade and to the raw materials of the world which are needed for their economic prosperity" can only be reasonably interpreted against the backdrop of the relations among the principal industrial powers in the 1930s and of the conflicts consequent upon the global economic crisis. It is not the disparities of today but the presumed sources of the interwar struggle between the "haves" and the "have-nots" that were to be corrected through the provision for greater equality of opportunity. So, too, the "freedom from want" pledged in the Atlantic Charter is to be interpreted in terms of domestic policies that would establish more just domestic social orders, rather than in terms of any international redistribution of wealth.

Similarly, the structure of the institutions to govern the postwar world can scarcely be interpreted as a departure from traditional patterns of inequality. The Bretton Woods institutions (the International Monetary Fund and the World Bank) closely reflect, in their voting arrangements as well as in other ways, the economic inequality of the participant states (an inequality that separated the United States from all other participants). These institutions were designed to reestablish, under American leadership, a liberal international economic order in place of the largely mercantilist system that had prevailed in the 1930s. The purpose of such order was to insure the free flow of trade and investment, whatever effects this might have on disparities of wealth among countries.* It is only in a later period that this purpose has been partially transformed to effect a greater equality of opportunity and even of condition.†

In the structure of the United Nations Charter, the reality of inequality is no less, despite the affirmation of the "equal rights . . . of nations large and small," the pledge to respect "the sovereign equality of all the members of the United Nations," and the voting provisions for the General Assembly. In the charter's original design of order, the feature of fundamental importance is the practically exclusive power and almost unlimited discretion conferred upon the Security Council—that is, upon the great powers—in providing for international peace and security. The charter faithfully reflected the collective hegemony the great powers were intended to exercise in the postwar world, a hegemony President Roosevelt insistently identified as "trusteeship."

Certainly, the declared assumption of the charter's principal framers was that the enforcement measures authorized by the organization were intended to preserve the legitimate interests of the individual member nations while at the same time preserving the broader community interest in maintaining international peace and order. Still, the charter afforded no assurance that the powers accorded the Security Council would be so employed as to give equal protection to all interests of all member states. The charter's design of order was made dependent on the condition that the great powers retain a basic identity of interests (a design that in itself clearly did not

---

* Once again, of course, the assumption was that a liberal international economic order would eventually operate to reduce such disparities, and that what was in the interests of the rich would also be in the interests of the poor.

† The World Bank's original function was to assist in reconstruction by offering loans at commercial rates. As one observer has written, "There was simply no conception of the vast needs of the less developed countries and of the role the Bank should play in them" (Richard N. Gardner, *Sterling-Dollar Diplomacy* [New York: McGraw-Hill, 1969], p. xxx). It was not until 1960, with the creation of the International Development Association, that a soft-loan facility became available to these less-developed areas. Even in the Fund, with regard to economic relations among the "haves," adoption of a more limited liquidity, as advocated by the U.S. and opposed by Britain, reflected the primacy of existing inequalities over the desire to minimize disparities and alleviate adjustment problems.

33

preclude acknowledgment of great-power spheres of influence). As long as this basic identity of interests was maintained, if the price of order was deemed by the great powers to necessitate the sacrifice of what otherwise would be regarded as the legitimate interests of states, there was little in the charter to prevent this sacrifice. Given the role and powers of the Security Council, the chief difference between the traditional balance-of-power system and the system of the charter is that the latter sought to make explicit and to legitimize what the former left rather obscure and never quite dared to legitimize.

If today we are to find in the United Nations the principal institutional expression of the demand for greater equality, we must do so in terms of what the organization has become and not in terms of what it was initially intended to be. The change from an instrument of the great powers to a forum in which the new states could press their claims begins in the late 1950s and coincides with events that suddenly gave the weak of the world unexpected significance. In part, this significance may be traced simply to the impact of the rapid decolonization that marked the years from the late 1940s through the early 1960s and to the very novelty of an international system that had achieved universality. Even in the absence of the cold war, this sudden appearance of a large number of new states would have aroused exaggerated expectations of their effect on world politics and, particularly, on great-power relations. In part, however, what gave special significance to the emergence of these states was a bipolar power structure and a concomitant hegemonial conflict that soon became coextensive with what was for the first time a universal international system.

In retrospect, the speed with which decolonization occurred seems only secondary in importance to the fact of its occurrence. Within a period of roughly fifteen years, formal inequalities of status had virtually disappeared, creating as a result as many states as had existed before the process began. Moreover, this achievement of formal equality was only the prelude to further claims to equality. The sudden attainment of political independence by so many peoples formed only the beginning of a challenge to inequality that continues to preoccupy us today—indeed, that preoccupies us today more than ever. Nor is this challenge confined to those peoples who until so recently were without formal equality. It has been taken up as well by peoples—in Latin America—who have long possessed formal equality but who have nevertheless been in a position of semi-dependence by virtue of their economic backwardness and political weakness. If we go beyond the literal meaning of "new," these latter states also may be considered among the "new states," judging by their claims and aspirations to an ever increasing measure of equality.*

The new egalitarianism must therefore be seen to stem in large measure from the very rapidity with which decolonization finally occurred. For the sudden transformation in status of so many peoples gave an initial momentum to a movement that still shows few signs of slowing down. Had decolonization taken place over a substantially longer period, the consequences in all likelihood would have been quite different. A few new states could have been gradually absorbed into the existing system with little perturbation. In time, inequalities of opportunity as well as of condition would surely have been challenged. Even so, such challenge would have been of a different magnitude and, it is not unreasonable to assume, would have taken a different form.

If only for these reasons, the contingent causes of the great change that came so quickly in the wake of World War II are important. To say this is not to detract from the significance of the deeper causes that eventually were bound to result in the breakup of empire. It is no

* It is for these reasons that in the ensuing discussion the term "new states" is used synonymously with "developing states." The term "Third World" is also used to denote the developing states, though growing disparities in income and wealth among these states have led some writers to distinguish between the Third and Fourth worlds, the latter comprising the very poor developing states. Finally, the terms "North" and "South" have appeared as shorthand expressions for differentiating between the developed states (capitalist and Communist) and the developing states. The ritual warning in using these expressions may be repeated here to the effect that the many disparities among the new states or the developing states or the Third World or the South ought not to be obscured by virtue of terminological conveniences.

doubt the case, as Geoffrey Barraclough has written, that "the European powers when they intervened in Asia and Africa, were caught in a dialectic of their own making; every action they took for the purpose of governing and developing the territories they had annexed made the maintenance of their own position more difficult, and there appears to have been no line of policy by which they could have escaped this fatal predicament." * In the same vein, another historian of empire's decline concludes that "the actual source of all decolonization movements lay in the process of colonization itself. The 'opening up of the world' by Europeans necessarily set in motion a process of emancipation which destroyed traditional social structures and led to the formation of 'new' societies and nations that had, at a given moment, to resist European dominance and demand the sovereign rights proclaimed by their teachers." †

These statements are unexceptionable as general explanations of the revolt against the imperialism of the West. At the same time, they do not and cannot account for the timing and manner of the breakup of empire. Fot this we must look, in part at least, to contingent causes, among which the most important was undoubtedly the Second World War. The profound causes of decolonization were apparent in the interwar period. Still, it is safe to say that in the absence of the war empires would not have come to an end when they did and in the manner they did. When the war broke out, the continued power of the European metropoles to prevail against independence movements was almost nowhere in serious doubt. When the war ended, there were very few areas in Asia where it was not in serious doubt. Only in Africa did it appear that empire still had a lease on life and that the process of decolonization might not be substantially completed before the end of the century, if then. Here, too, it soon became apparent that the effects of the war—in Africa, in the metropoles, and in the international position of the colonial powers—had been to telescope developments that in the mid-1940s still appeared, and not implausibly so, to be quite distant.

* Barraclough, *Introduction to Contemporary History,* p. 160.
† Rudolf Von Albertini, *Decolonization,* p. 28.

A New International System?

The war did not result in an absolute decline in the power of the European metropoles. But this was perhaps the least important factor in accounting for the rapid postwar decolonization. Of crucial significance was the dramatic decline in the relative power of these states. In Asia this decline cannot be understood apart from the defeat and humiliation suffered by the Western powers at the hands of the Japanese. Once before, at the beginning of the century, Japan had set an example for Asian peoples in defeating Russia. But this earlier precedent was modest in comparison with the Japanese victories over the Western powers in the early stages of World War II. It is generally acknowledged that the effective end of empire in Asia for Great Britain came with the surrender of British forces to the Japanese at Singapore in February 1942.* Elsewhere, as in French Indochina and the Dutch East Indies, Japanese victories foreshadowed the imminent end of Western rule. Given the vast populations over which this rule was exercised, it could only be effectively maintained either by the self-assurance of a seldom challenged authority or by the commitment of very large forces together with a willingness to use those forces whenever and however necessary. The victorious Japanese sweep in Asia, together with the encouragement Japan gave for its own purposes to nationalist movements in occupied territories, insured that the former alternative could never again be successfully employed. If empire was to survive for even a brief season in Asia, it could do so only by choosing the latter alternative.

Given their relative decline in power, a policy of hanging on to empire by means of an open-ended commitment to suppress independence movements was simply not a practicable alternative in such critical cases as India and the East Indies. Britain and the Netherlands, even if they had been so disposed, could not have maintained their respective positions save at ruinous price, and then with no greater prospect than one of marginally postponing the inevitable. It was not a practicable alternative for the further reason that in the aftermath of the war there developed in the metropoles a greater

* This is a retrospective judgment. At the time, the significance of Singapore was grasped by only a minority of observers.

unwillingness to use military power in order to maintain empire. This unwillingness was not everywhere apparent in the same degree. It was markedly greater in Britain than in France, perhaps in part because the British, unlike the French, did not have to seek psychological compensation in their colonies for defeat in war.* In part, however, it was greater because the conflict between empire and liberty had always been posed more sharply and insistently in Great Britain. From the outset, the British had justified empire as a preparation for independence—that is, for self-government of the political community—and not, as in the case of France, a promise of individual freedom and equal status for inhabitants of the colonies and the metropole alike. In the circumstances following World War II, Britain could deny independence to India only by betraying promises made in the war years and by making a farce of this larger justification for empire. Once independence was granted to India (and to Burma and Ceylon as well), the fatal precedent was set and the British found it increasingly difficult to respond with force to demands for independence elsewhere. Although Britain's justification for empire ultimately made the British morally vulnerable to claims for independence, it also made it easier for them to abandon empire when their decline in power left no real alternative. In most cases, they could retire with relative good grace because they could persuade themselves that they were leaving with their historic task having been largely accomplished and not simply because they were confronted by *force majeure*.

More important than moral compunctions over the use of force in accounting for the end of empire was the rapidly changing nature of Western societies in the postwar years. There is no need to undertake here a specification of this change. It is sufficient to note that the transformation that did occur removed those last vestiges of traditional society sympathetic to the enterprise of empire. It is significant that Portugal, the one Western European colonial power remaining

---

* One must add to this the British belief that the informal ties of Commonwealth would still reap many of the benefits for Britain that former colonial states had done (though without the cost of empire).

outside the change encompassing the rest of Europe, did not abandon empire until the 1970s. Elsewhere, the characteristics of industrialized societies, increasingly oriented around consumption and welfare goals, were increasingly inimical to the demands of empire. It is true that for a time, during the 1950s, France and Belgium nevertheless seem determined to hold on to empire in Africa. In fact, this determination was rapidly eroding under a domestic opinion that no longer found in empire a source of prestige and that no longer wished to bear the costs of an enterprise that appeared to return few, if any, tangible benefits.*

This determination also eroded before an independence movement that seemed to gather ever greater momentum as it went along. In sustaining this momentum, the power of example proved very important. Nor did it matter that examples were often drawn from different continents and ignored the great differences of condition in which independence was sought. Western critics of sudden decolonization in Africa often pointed to the evident differences between decolonization in most of Asia and decolonization in most of Africa. Whatever its merits, the argument was simply vain in the face of a movement that by the middle to late 1950s had developed a momentum that could not be checked. In the United Nations, the strength of the movement was reflected by the growing defensiveness of those states still possessing colonies in a forum that was regularly and effectively employed by the newly emancipated to arraign colonialism. The world organization, moreover, was employed not only to arraign the colonial powers before the bar of world opinion but eventually to legitimize measures—including forcible measures—to bring colonialism to an end.†

---

* Of course, a special case arises where a substantial portion of a colonial power's population has settled in the occupied territories. The French attitude toward Algeria cannot be appreciated without taking into account the million French that had settled in Algeria. Nor, for that matter, can be the Portuguese attitude toward Angola and Mozambique.

† This, at least, was the implication the new states read into the General Assembly's Declaration on the Granting of Independence to Colonial Countries and Peoples of December 12, 1960, which stipulated that "all peoples have the right to self-

In the vast process of decolonization, the United States necessarily played a role, for it was by any calculation the predominant power in the international system. In varying degree, the major colonial powers were dependent on it, and in the years immediately following the war critically so. Yet the role of the United States in decolonization is easily, and often, exaggerated. It is commonly forgotten today that despite the traditional American support of the principle of self-determination and despite the well-publicized differences between Roosevelt and Churchill during the war years over the fate of the British empire, the American view on decolonization was a cautious one in World War II. It was not part of the American scheme for the postwar order that the colonial empires should simply be disbanded by granting colonies independence. On the contrary, the prevailing view was that most colonies were not yet ready for independence and would not be ready for a considerable period of time. The initial American plan, rejected by the British, to place all colonies under United Nations trusteeship was not a covert scheme for rapid decolonization but a plan for avoiding postwar colonial rivalries.

Although in the immediate postwar period, as before, the United States proclaimed its anti-colonialism, in action this country was more cautious and conservative than in word. It did refuse in 1945 to extend to France military aid intended for use in Indochina, though this was perhaps as indicative of a general lack of sympathy for the French as it was indicative of anti-colonialism. Elsewhere in Asia, the United States welcomed the British grant of independence to India, Burma, and Ceylon. On the other hand, it did not oppose in any way the Dutch effort to hang on in Indonesia until a very late date, when that effort appeared certain to fail. With respect to Africa—south of the Sahara, at any rate—decolonization was regarded as a still distant prospect.

Quite apart from the subsequent impact of the cold war, which gave rise to "necessities" of its own, it is not unfair to interpret America's post-World War II anti-colonialism in much the same way

_____

determination." The declaration does not directly define those (peoples) who are the subject of this right.

as Wilson's anti-colonialism of a generation before. Indirectly, the United States did promote decolonization, if only by virtue of its professed sympathies. It may of course be argued that to leave the matter there neglects the importance of a policy of denying assistance to the efforts of the colonial powers to hold on to empire, and so it does. But this argument does no more than affirm what few would care to deny—that American policy was not pro-colonial. The refusal to prop up empire, even that of allies, is scarcely an impressive test of anti-colonialism. Indeed, in the decade or so following the war it is difficult to find an example that bears out an anti-colonialism that goes beyond the "power of denial" through passivity. The American reaction in 1956 to the Anglo-French intervention at Suez perhaps comes closest as an exception to this general pattern, and even this apparent exception must be in part accounted for by reasons other than anti-colonialism.

In time, the American dilemma of maintaining good relations with its major European allies while retaining influence with the emergent and new states of Asia and Africa was largely resolved simply through the virtual disappearance of the conditions that had given rise to the dilemma. The French decision to grant independence to Algeria marks the end of this period. In the last great chapter in the brief history of decolonization, the European states—Portugal apart—were only too willing to divest themselves of their remaining African colonies. Given this disposition, the United States could openly support the emancipation of peoples that heretofore had been thought least able to sustain political independence. The irony of this final reckoning, in which those least prepared for independence were virtually pushed into a status of formal equality, was not missed. By the end of the 1950s, however, it was much too late to apply criteria of independence that subject peoples had never accepted and that the rising number of new states were less disposed than ever to consider in the case of remaining colonies. Nor did the United States entertain any intention of jeopardizing its relations with those who had become a major stake in the cold war by questioning the abandon with which new states were created in Africa.

IV

It has become a part of the conventional wisdom of this period that the cold war played an important role in forcing the pace of decolonization.* When applied to the all-important earlier phase of decolonization, there is very little evidence to sustain this view. The fall of empire in Asia came, for the most part, in the late 1940s and was the result of circumstances that had almost no relation to the gathering East-West conflict. If anything, a case of sorts may be made for the opposite view that the emergence of the cold war served to prolong empire in Asia. Certainly, it is difficult to see the United States extending the substantial military aid to France that it did from 1950, in support of the French effort in Indochina, had it not been for the cold war. Equally, it is difficult to see the United States later stepping in to fill the position left by the French had it not been for the policy of containing communism in Asia.

In general, the view that the cold war was important in speeding the decolonization process rests on the assumptions that it worked to encourage independence movements while seriously constraining efforts that otherwise would have been taken by the colonial powers to put these movements down. The cold war did undoubtedly serve to encourage a number of independence movements. It did so if only because it freed the Soviet Union from restraints it might have been expedient to observe in the absence of intense rivalry with the West. Indeed, in the years immediately following World War II, and before the cold war had become set, the Soviet Union had observed on more than one occasion surprising restraint in exploiting colonial issues. This restraint was abandoned by the early 1950s, however, and the Soviet Union's support of independence movements became un-

---

* "I think we can explain the rapidity and extensiveness of postwar decolonization only by reference to the disunity and rivalry of the major powers, their Cold War-inspired urge to outdo each other in bloc-building, and their atomically-inspired caution about resorting to the use of their military power" (Inis L. Claude, Jr., *The Changing United Nations* [New York: Random House, 1967], p. 51). Claude's view is a representative one.

disguised and, in a number of cases, substantial in terms of aid rendered. In turn, the United States was often driven by its competition with the Soviet Union to manifest greater support for independence movements than would otherwise have been the case. Despite these considerations, the principal determinant by far of the pace of decolonization was the extent to which the metropole was able and willing to slow this pace. Neither ability nor willingness appear to have been materially affected by the necessities of the cold war. In the case of Britain, a substantial and prolonged commitment of military power to hold back decolonization would have subjected the economy to intolerable strain and was, in any event, a political impossibility for any postwar government. In the case of France, the cold war formed no more than a marginal consideration, if that, in the effort to hold on in Indochina and North Africa. And when Britain, France, and Belgium decided to let go in Africa, the cold war still remained subordinate to their determination to rid themselves of what had become an economic burden and a persisting political stigma in the eyes of all the new states.

It is another matter to argue that the cold war played an important role in the immediate post-colonial evolution of many new states and that it did so by influencing the assessment these states made of the international system and of their significance in that system. This result followed from the very character of the hegemonial conflict that attended the early years of the new states. The pervasiveness of the cold war was matched by its intensity. A characteristic feature of the conflict was the tendency to make almost any discrete issue into a symbol of the whole and to relate almost any conflict of interest to the underlying and ultimate conflict of interest. In these circumstances, the new states of the Third World took on an importance for the superpowers they would not otherwise have enjoyed. Although almost any feasible shift in their political allegiance could not have decisively altered the respective power positions of the United States and the Soviet Union, it was nonetheless assumed that the global balance of power might well depend upon the ultimate disposition of the underdeveloped nations. In fact, once the cold war moved from

Europe to Asia, and to the Third World generally, conventional balance-of-power calculations became increasingly irrelevant to the major protagonists. What moved the latter was not so much a fear for their conventional security interests—though this fear was never absent—as a fear that they might become irrelevant to the majority of humanity comprising the Third World. It was this prospect of a diminishing influence that led to the vision (or nightmare), which persisted for more than a decade, of an America beleaguered in a hostile world that had chosen the example of communism.

Although the cold war gave many of the states of the Third World a salience and leverage they would otherwise not have enjoyed, it also limited considerably their independence and freedom of action. Conversely, although the decline in intensity of the cold war after the mid-1960s increased the level of independence of these states, it did so largely because the great cold-war protagonists attached a decreasing significance to an interest they had earlier deemed crucial. In part, they did so simply for the reason that in the wake of the Cuban missile crisis, and the dangers that crisis illuminated, they had partially and almost imperceptibly turned away from a view of their rivalry that previously had given it an almost completely hegemonic cast. In part, perhaps, they did so out of a sense of fatigue as well as out of a growing realization that the contest could not have a decisive outcome, particularly in the area that the cold war had increasingly centered on. The struggle over the Third World had been primarily a struggle for political allegiance and influence, not territorial control or conquest. But the reliability of political allegiance and influence in the absence of more traditional means of control was increasingly placed in question. Thus, what had once appeared as a vital and manageable stake in the cold war took on an elusive and questionable character.

It is not without irony that the decrease in the significance to the two great powers of the Third World states coincided with the rise in the demands of the latter for a greater measure of equality. Although by the middle to late 1960s the restraints imposed upon the new states by the cold war had clearly begun to recede, the burdens an increased measure of independence imposed upon political leaders of these states had just as clearly not receded. However persistent many Third World governments had been in their criticism of the cold war, the attention they had received as a result of that conflict had assuaged deep anxieties over their very viability as states. If the cold war restricted their freedom of action, it also gave them a much needed sense of importance and worth. This latter sense was probably of greater moment to governing elites than fears—real or simply professed—that the cold war threatened their independence, for despite the restraints it imposed, the cold war provided a psychic confirmation of independence.

In retrospect, then, the cold war may be seen as having afforded not so much the occasion for an otherwise unexpectedly rapid decolonization as a stimulus to demands for greater equality on the part of the new and developing states. Indeed, no sooner had the first revolt against the West been consummated than the second began. Nevertheless, the common view at the close of the 1960s was that the Third World formed, for the most part, an area of marginal significance in world politics. Even those who objected to this view, and to what they saw as its manifestations in the Nixon foreign policy, did so more out of hope that the developed and capitalist states might be induced to acknowledge a responsibility to improve the lot of the developing nations than out of conviction that the latter might somehow compel the former to do so. No doubt, this view was an exaggerated—and, as it turned out, short-lived—reaction to what appeared as an excessive preoccupation in the 1960s with the Third World, a preoccupation that was held largely responsible for the disastrous intervention in Vietnam. We had failed to see that the world—developed and underdeveloped alike—had become pluralistic. Although a pluralistic world might be far more complicated than the world of the classic cold war, it was nevertheless held to be a much safer world. Interpreted in essence as the triumph of nationalism, pluralism in the prevailing view meant that Communist expansion no longer carried the threat to America it once did. Pluralism also meant that the prospect of Communist expansion had dramatically declined. With that decline, the importance of the Third World declined as well. Contrary to the radical explanation that we were in Vietnam because the greater stake in the conflict was continued access to indispensable raw materials on Western terms, the prevailing view became that we were in Vietnam because we had misunderstood the changes that had taken place in the world. Indeed, the argument went, we had never really understood the Third World at all. John Kenneth Galbraith summarized the new understanding of Third World states in these terms:

> They are poor and rural. . . . For the appreciable future they will so remain. Even by the crudest power calculus, military or economic, such nations have no vital relation to the economic or strategic position of the developed countries. They do supply raw materials. But even here the typical observation concerns not their power as sources of such supply, but rather their weakness as competitive hewers of wood in the markets of the industrially advanced countries.*

With the advantage of hindsight, we can see what Galbraith passed over: that the supply of raw materials might not always be in excess of demand, that at least some of the "hewers of wood" might choose to combine rather than to compete, and—above all—that the heretofore weak might achieve a "vital relation" to the strong should the latter, for whatever reasons, prove unable or disinclined to make use of their strength. The Galbraith view assumed the developing states would continue to form the passive and dependent periphery they had always formed. Though no longer formally unequal, their new status would not serve to alter the basic pattern of relationships they had hitherto entertained with the developed and capitalist countries. Indeed, what modest leverage they had momentarily enjoyed by virtue of the intense hegemonial contest between the United States and the Soviet Union would erode. With the decline of the classic cold war, and of the excesses this conflict had brought, the subordinate position of the Third World in the postwar order would be reaffirmed.

* John Kenneth Galbraith, "Plain Lessons of a Bad Decade," *Foreign Policy* 1 (Winter 1970–71): 37.

A New International System?

But the postwar order was itself breaking down during these years. Largely the creation of America, this order rested upon and reflected America's continued military, political, and economic supremacy. Even in the absence of Vietnam, the decline of the classic cold war was bound to challenge this supremacy by eroding the cohesiveness of the American-led alliance system. No longer perceiving the threat to their security they had once perceived, America's major allies were no longer willing to accept American leadership in the manner they once had. They were no longer willing to do so because the question of American leadership now revolved largely around economic issues, which, to the degree they were dealt with in isolation from military-security issues, could not give rise to the compulsions of yesterday. On the contrary, economic issues more often than not revealed growing conflicts of interest while providing no readily available means of resolving these conflicts. Although the earlier compulsions of the cold war were increasingly discounted, the disparities in economic capability as between America and her major allies had narrowed. Given these changes, many conflicts of interest between America and Europe (and Japan) now went unresolved, since neither the incentives nor the power preponderance required to resolve them were present.

The intervention in Vietnam also challenged America's supremacy and thus the foundations of the postwar order. It did so as perhaps no other event had since the close of World War II. By the end of the 1960s it was apparent that there would be no American victory in Vietnam, indeed, that American power either would not or simply could not be employed to stave off what, at best, would be a thinly disguised defeat. Whereas the precise impact throughout the Third World of the American failure in Vietnam remains a matter of uncertainty and controversy, it seems only reasonable to conclude that the effects were considerable. If the argument of liberal critics of the war were pursued, Vietnam demonstrated above all the triumphant force of nationalism in the Third World. But the argument, even if well-taken, did not affect the point that this triumph of nationalism might still be seen by the new states as a successful challenge to the foundations on which the American inspired postwar order rested. The radical position on Vietnam might be very misleading as an explanation of the origins of American intervention yet close to the mark in its calculation of the consequences of defeat. Given the reaction of the new states to America's failure in Vietnam, earlier radical projections of the consequences of defeat, though exaggerated, were still remarkably prophetic.

It was in these general circumstances marking the early 1970s, circumstances in which American power became increasingly questioned both at home and abroad, that the challenge to inequality by the new states achieved salience and took on a new importance. In fact, this challenge had slowly but steadily gathered momentum throughout the preceding decade. It had done so in international forums where the increasing acceptance of the "one state, one vote" rule gave the small and weak an influence they had not possessed in the traditional system, dominated as it was by customary practices that reflected a consensus of the strong. It found expression in the United Nations Conference on Trade and Development (UNCTAD), initiated in 1964, which sought substantial change in the international economic system. In general, the 1960s witnessed an emergent political equality attended by a rising demand for a greater measure of protection for the economic interests of the underdeveloped states and by the insistence that the historically disadvantaged be given preferential treatment in order to achieve greater equality of opportunity and, finally, to narrow existing inequalities of income and wealth.

Even so, the challenge to inequality by the new states required a dramatic event—an apparent sudden breakthrough—to give it the significance it has acquired today. That event, as everyone knows, occurred in the late fall and early winter of 1973–74, when the Organization of Petroleum Exporting Countries (OPEC) raised the price of oil fourfold without provoking an effective reaction—forcible or otherwise—on the part of the developed and capitalist nations. In thus dictating the price that the rich and poor alike have since had to pay for oil, the OPEC cartel succeeded beyond the wildest dreams of its founding fathers. And in so doing it was only to be expected that the action of the oil cartel would be seen by its supporters in the Third World, and elsewhere as well, as the beginning of a new chapter in world history. More important than the amount of wealth of the industrialized world siphoned off at one stroke by the decision to multiply the price of oil is the historic reversal presumably represented by the decision itself. In one sympathetic interpretation, this decision of the oil exporting countries is seen as putting ''an end to an era which had begun with what the West calls the 'great discoveries.' For the first time since Vasco da Gama, mastery over a fundamental decision in a crucial area of the economic policy of the centre countries escaped their grasp as certain peripheral countries wrested it from them.'' *

Is this interpretation little more than rhetorical flourish and artless exaggeration? In the claim that the peripheral countries ''wrested'' power from the center countries, rather than being almost invited by the latter to assume mastery over a fundamental decision, do we have good history or merely wishful thinking? These questions are doubtless of interest to the dispassionate observer. At the same time, their relevance to the course of the contemporary challenge to inequality may prove marginal. It is easy to demonstrate that no other Third World commodity cartel, and perhaps no feasible combination of such cartels, can confer the wealth and growing power presently enjoyed by the oil cartel. This being the case, it is equally easy to conclude that the expectations generated by OPEC have no solid basis in economic reality. The view of a Michael Manley, the Jamaican Prime Minister—''that OPEC, along with its younger cousins like the International Bauxite Association, have changed the fundamental equations of economic power as decisively as did the Industrial Revolution'' †—has accordingly been dismissed by many observers as an economic fantasy.

---

* *The 1975 Dag Hammarskjöld Report on Development and International Cooperation,* prepared on the occasion of the Seventh Special Session of the United Nations General Assembly (New York, September 1–12, 1975), p. 6.

† *New York Times,* October 13, 1975, p. 14.

Yet the deeper meaning of OPEC, intuition alone suggests, cannot be measured simply by these considerations. The action of the oil cartel is significant above all because of the manner in which it has been perceived by the Southern states and because of the expectations this perception has engendered. In consequence, an extraordinary added momentum has been given to the demands of the developing states for greater equality. To be sure, the action of the cartel is also significant in pointing to the many conflicts of interest among the new states. Given normal expectations of state behavior, a number of these conflicts can be expected to persist and even deepen if for no other reason than as a result of markedly different rates of development. The relative indifference with which the major OPEC states have viewed the devastating effects of oil prices on many developing countries is an indication, if one were needed, of the conflicts of interest that are bound to arise among the Southern states. The oil crisis, in addition to putting to rest the romantic notion that the new states would lead the way to humanity's moral regeneration, affords apparent vindication of the view that "the South" does not exist in the sense that it was widely seen to exist only a decade ago.

But these considerations do not deny the point that the OPEC states have set an example others will try to emulate, though in different ways and on a more modest scale. Communal solidarity is not a prerequisite to common grievances that express themselves in claims to greater equality. Nor, for that matter, is the presence of conflicting interests a bar to the pursuit of interests that are still perceived as shared by most governments of the South. The rather disconcerting truth is that the reactions of Southern victims of oil prices have been almost as astonishing in their way as the reactions of Northern victims. A large literature on what sociologists term "relative deprivation" would have led us to expect the Southern countries to show intense resentment toward the sudden riches and new status of the major OPEC states, particularly in view of the lack of concern the latter have shown over the effects their actions have had on the world's poor. It may be a mixture of fear and hope that prevents this resentment from becoming fully manifest. Then again, however, it may be, and in all probability is, the persistence of grievances and interests that are still held in common despite feelings of resentment. To the extent that it is the persistence of commonly held grievances and interests, the response of the developed states to OPEC actions has clearly not served to discourage the claims of the new states. If anything, this response has given such claims greater impetus.

V

The claims of the new states have not fallen on deaf ears in the developed and capitalist states. On the contrary, what is extraordinary about the contemporary challenge to international inequality is not only the challenge itself but the response it has elicited among liberal elites in the Western industrialized states. The attitudes of these elites toward international inequalities have altered, and—on the surface at least—quite markedly so. Indeed, so apparently pervasive has this alteration been that the articulate few who do not share it are seen as eccentric, if not perverse. Yet until only recently an outlook now considered virtually incontestable would itself have been viewed as eccentric. Writing of the sudden awareness of the "world poverty problem" and of the emergent conviction of a "collective responsibility" on the part of the rich nations for alleviating the plight of the world's poor, Gunnar Myrdal declares that "we have been living through one of history's most abrupt reversals of political climate." * Myrdal associates this reversal not only with elite opinion but with public opinion generally in the Western nations. In fact, there is little evidence for asserting so broad an association and a good deal of evidence that points to a quite different conclusion. At the same time, it is apparent that among the regnant intellectual elites of the developed states of the West we have been witnessing a

* Gunnar Myrdal, "The World Poverty Problem," *Britannica Book of the Year 1972,* (Chicago: *Encyclopedia Britannica,* 1972), p. 22.

change in attitude that, for the time being at least, is extraordinary. A new political sensibility has arisen with respect to international inequalities of income and wealth. Provided it were to persist, and eventually extend to publics and governments, the consequences could be momentous.

The origins of the new political sensibility may be traced back to the middle to late 1960s. It is in this period that liberal intellectual elites in the West become increasingly preoccupied, in a way they had not been before, with the issue of international inequalities of income and wealth (it is in the same period that they become increasingly preoccupied with domestic inequalities of income and wealth). And it is in this period that the conviction develops of a duty on the part of the rich nations to reduce such inequalities. Those who, like Myrdal, find the "new idea of collective responsibility" emerging in the years following World War II have taken the exhortations of no more than a handful for what was only later to become a substantial group and an increasingly pervasive intellectual climate.

There are of course elements of continuity between these earlier years and the period of interest here. Nevertheless, the elements of continuity are clearly outweighed by the elements of change. In its emphasis on equality as the principal moral imperative of our time,* in its insistence on the duty of the rich to redress global inequalities,† and in its conviction that inequalities of income and wealth represent the most serious long-term threat to world peace, the new political sensibility may be distinguished from views that prevailed during the years of the classic cold war. Whereas earlier views were inevitably influenced by the hegemonic conflict and the security-power necessities it imposed—or, at any rate, was thought at the time to impose—the new political sensibility is clearly a post-cold war outlook. It is so

* Zbigniew Brzezinski finds that "equality is becoming the most powerful moral imperative of our time, thus paralleling the appeal of the concept of liberty during the 19th century." So, too, he finds that "the problem of the less developed nations is the moral problem of our time" ("U.S. Foreign Policy: The Search for Focus," *Foreign Affairs*, 51 [July 1973]: 717, 726).

† "The developed nations . . . must do more to promote a least minimal equity in the distribution of wealth among nations" (Robert S. McNamara, Address to the Board of Governors, the World Bank, September 25, 1972).

in the narrow and literal sense of regarding the hegemonic rivalry that once dominated world politics as largely spent (and, to the degree that rivalry persists, as no longer of central significance). It is so in the broader sense of seeing the cold war as a response to forces that even at the time had become increasingly atavistic and that certainly no longer accurately characterize the international scene. The period of the classic cold war, then, was the last great manifestation of the old politics, with its parochial interests, its obsession with national power, its hierarchical ordering of states, and its reliance on forcible methods. In contrast, the new political sensibility proclaims a politics of interdependence for a world that must cope with problems the nature and dimensions of which will no longer yield to the particularistic methods of the past, and surely not to the forcible methods of the past. In place of a world in which the hierarchical ordering of states seemed natural and inevitable, interdependence holds out the promise—as another sanguine analyst puts it—of "a world in which nobody is in charge."

Although it is apparent that the rise of the new political sensibility is a response to the decline of the cold war, it is equally apparent that this outlook must be traced to the disappointment bordering on despair over the results of development strategies and projections confidently set forth in the 1950s and early 1960s. With few exceptions, these optimistic projections did not materialize, though for reasons—the rapid growth of population apart—that are still a matter of dispute. Of relevance here is that a growing despair over achieving the goal of converging per-capita growth rates coincided in the early 1970s not only with an increased militance on the part of the new states but with the new-found concern in the West that the process of industrial growth itself was no longer to be taken for granted, whether because of the constraints imposed by limited natural resources or because of the constraints imposed by the growth process itself on the various forms of pollution.

Thus, what had once been seen as a story that would have in the not too distant future a happy ending for the new states, and that would involve only the mildest of sacrifice—if sacrifice at all—on the part of the developed states, was suddenly seen as a story that might have a very unhappy ending indeed, and not only for the poor countries. The most striking presentation of the dark night that all too likely awaits us has been made by Robert Heilbroner. In Heilbroner's words, "whether we are unable to sustain growth or unable to tolerate it, there can be no doubt that a radically different future beckons." * That future does not portend cooperation but rather intense conflict between the rich and the poor of the world. "We are entering a period," Heilbroner concludes, "in which rapid population growth, the presence of obliterative weapons, and dwindling resources will bring international tensions to dangerous levels for an extended period. Indeed, there seems no reason for these levels of danger to subside unless population equilibrium is achieved and some rough measure of equity reached in the distribution of wealth among nations, either by great increase in the output of the underdeveloped world or by a massive redistribution of wealth from the richer to the poorer lands." † Little in the Heilbroner analysis suggests the likelihood of reaching such an equitable arrangement by either route. On the contrary, given the world he projects, the state, both in the developed and underdeveloped worlds, must be expected to exhibit more separatist and self-centered behavior than in the past.

If the Heilbroner assessment—and similar assessments—form one reaction to a world divided between rich and poor, and confronted with the twin prospects of resource scarcities and pollution as limits to growth, the new political sensibility may be seen as another and, on the face of it, altogether different reaction. Whereas the Heilbroner assessment points to increased conflict between rich and poor, to "wars of redistribution" or "preemptive seizures," the new political sensibility emphasizes the prospect—indeed, the necessity—for greater cooperation among nations precisely because of the dangers that confront them all if they do not acknowledge their interdependence through cooperative arrangements that, among other things,

* Robert L. Heilbroner, *An Inquiry Into the Human Prospect* (New York: W. W. Norton, 1974), p. 94.
† Heilbroner, *Inquiry Into the Human Prospect,* p. 127.

must clearly reduce present disparities in standards of living. To Heilbroner such arrangements appear very unlikely, given human nature and the behavior of collectives; at least they appear unlikely in the absence of catastrophe—whether social or natural—which would force us to mend our present ways. The new political sensibility, however, finds in these alternatives to interdependence precisely the incentives required to effect needed change. Thus, what are for Heilbroner despotic forces—above all, the despotism of the industrial mode of production—relentlessly driving us ever closer to perdition are to the new political sensibility benevolently despotic forces that will ultimately lead—and are leading—humanity to true community.*

The new political sensibility thus proceeds from the acute awareness of a condition that is considered at once politically dangerous and morally intolerable. In later pages we will review expressions of this conviction. Suffice it to say here that the conviction of the political and moral hazards presumably inherent in an interdependent world that remains sharply divided between rich and poor has attained the status almost of a received truth. This argument, it is true, does not prevent a substantial measure of disagreement among the adherents of this received truth, who—if, on the whole, of broadly liberal persuasion—still represent considerable diversity of view. The absence of consensus on the scope of the duty to reduce present disparities in income and wealth clearly does not extend to the point

* Despite the apparent disparities in these reactions, they may nevertheless reflect a deeper identity of view, since if men can only be persuaded that a continuance of their present ways must issue in catastrophe, they may change after all. In this sense, current despair may mask a deeper optimism, particularly if—as in Heilbroner's analysis—the period of acute danger is still a generation or two away. In the meantime, "the myopia that confines the present vision of men to the short-term future," to use Heilbroner's words, may yet be changed. Indeed, there is even a residual optimism in Heilbroner's view that we must let things get worse, much worse, before we can reasonably expect them to get better. Thus, Heilbroner's argument that "the outlook is for what we may call 'convulsive change'—change forced upon us by external events rather than by conscious choice, by catastrophe rather than by calculation"—is not as pessimistic as it appears. For the results of such convulsive change—though brutal—"are apt to prove effective in changing our attitudes as well as our actions. . . ." Even here, redemption is possible, though only after men have suffered sufficiently.

of principle itself; that is, to the point of questioning whether there is in principle a duty of the rich to reduce such disparities, even though the fulfillment of this duty will require sacrifice. Still less does it extend to what is commonly taken as the core meaning of the duty the rich have toward the poor, which is to insure minimal subsistence to all. That those who have should share with those who have not is considered unchallengeable.*

The new political sensibility accordingly proclaims a collective responsibility of universal application that heretofore has been applied only within the state and then only in this century (and in the United States only in this generation). In doing so, a parallel is drawn between the growth of equality within the domestic societies of the West and the greater society of states. In this view, what we are witnessing in international society is a historical development that, in its broad outlines, we have already experienced in domestic societies. In a world that becomes increasingly interdependent with each passing day, and that is no longer divided between the subjects of history and those who until recently were its mere objects, the processes that have characterized the internal development of the more advanced societies cannot be contained at the boundaries of the state. Some years ago an international jurist articulated the parallel that has come to form a central tenet of the new political sensibility:

A clear parallel can be drawn between the sociological development of the international and the national community. . . . Between the national and the international process of democracy there exists a connection. It is no mere accident that, after the supremacy and hegemony of the Western world, universalism in the community of nations was accepted once the process of democratization had been completed in the Western democracies.†

* The opening words of the above sentence are a paraphrase of the oft-quoted sentence that appeared in the report of the Pearson Commission: "The simplest answer to the question [why the rich should concern themselves with the plight of the poor] is the moral one: that it is only right for those who have to share with those who have not" (*Partners in Development: Report of the Commission on International Development* [United Nations, 1969], p. 8). A stimulating review and analysis of this and similar expressions is found in Theodore A. Sumberg, *Foreign Aid as Moral Obligation,* The Washington Papers I (Beverly Hills: Sage Publications, 1973).

† B. V. A. Röling, *International Law in an Expanded World* (Amsterdam: Djambatan, 1960), p. 56. Thus Röling sees international law proceeding from the law of

A New International System?

It is not difficult to see why this parallel has proved attractive. It responds to the persuasion of the "spill-over" effects of advanced societies; that is, to the presumed tendency of such societies to project abroad their deeper tendencies at home. Thus a society that moves toward greater internal equality will, in this view, eventually move toward the goal of greater equality abroad. This will be so particularly in an increasingly interdependent world yet one in which the disparity between the conditions of domestic and international life is both marked and apparent. Then, too, the parallel drawn between domestic and international society is found to draw considerable support from recent history. Reflecting the development of the more influential domestic societies, the conclusion seems only reasonable that "the world community is bound to become a welfare community, just as the nation state became a welfare state." *

VI

It is often assumed that there is a marked affinity between the new political sensibility entertained in the West today and the new egalitarianism entertained by the elites of the new states. In some respects, this assumption is well-taken. Both look to a significant shift of income and wealth. Both find this shift increasingly imposed upon the industrialized states by developments that have exposed the growing vulnerability of these states to disruption by the developing

---

freedom to the law of protection to the law of welfare (and beyond this, to the law of social and economic planning).

* Röling, Ibid. In 1971 Barbara Ward expressed confidence that the rich countries, "having accepted the principle of 'the general welfare' at home, . . . were ready to apply it to the whole family of man" (*The Widening Gap* [New York: Columbia Univ. Press, 1971], p. 13). A 1972 Brookings Institution reassessment of international economic relations declared: "The same motivation that leads the more advanced regions within a country to alleviate poverty in the less advanced may well be extended to the far deeper disparities that exist among different regions of the world" (*A Tripartite Report by Thirteen Experts* [Washington, D.C.: The Brookings Institution, 1972], p. 4).

countries. In other respects, however, there are marked divergencies between the new political sensibility and the new egalitarianism. Whereas the former projects a world in which the role of the sovereign state will decline, the latter projects a world in which sovereign states will occupy the role they have occupied in the past, and perhaps an even more important role. A global redistribution of income and wealth, according to the new egalitarianism, will mark a new beginning in history. Even so, this new beginning is not that foreshadowed by the new political sensibility, for redistribution will be largely effected by, and in the name of, states. The shift in power expected by the new egalitarianism to attend a shift in wealth is not identified with a change in the "essence" of power, just as a sought-after change in the present international hierarchy is not mistaken for the disappearance of hierarchy.

In large part, the new egalitarianism resembles nothing so much as the old equality. If international society is on the threshold of a new era, it is not apparent in the commitment of the new states to an interdependence that precludes the freedom of action states have habitually claimed in the name of their sovereign equality. Western observers may find a contradiction between the need for a more egalitarian international system—a need that presumably arises from a growing interdependence—and the insistence upon the state's undiminished sovereignty, but the elites of the new and developing countries do not share this outlook. On the contrary, for the latter it is the complete independence and sovereignty of the state that forms the most important—certainly the most emphasized—feature of the new egalitarianism. Interdependence is not seen as a means for drawing the sharp teeth of sovereignty but as an opportunity for obtaining maximum concessions from those states that possess a disproportionate share of the world's wealth and power.

Thus the principal purpose of the new economic order the developing states have articulated in recent years is not to consolidate an interdependence that progressively restricts the freedom of action of all states. It is, rather, the other way around. "The true meaning of interdependence," the 1975 Lima Declaration of Non-Aligned

Countries asserts, "[must] reflect unequivocally the common commitment to build the New International Economic Order." But the commitment to build the new international economic order is not one that is interpreted to limit in any significant way the sovereignty of the developing states. This is above all the case with respect to those activities of the state that traditionally have been considered to fall within its "domestic jurisdiction." The new states, with unwearying insistence, have reiterated that the international order, based on the sovereign equality of states, must accord to every state the unrestricted right to determine its own course of political, economic, and social development. The "full permanent sovereignty of every state over its natural resources and all economic activities," to use the words of the U.N. General Assembly's 1974 Declaration on the Establishment of a New International Economic Order, is an "inalienable right," the exercise of which is not to be subject to any external "economic, political, or other types of coercion."

This emphasis on interpreting equality largely as the absence of restraint upon the state's freedom of action has been repeatedly explained as the expected reaction to a long history of domination and inequality. A marked sensitivity to what is seen as the infringement of independence presumably reflects not only the experience of the past but anxieties over identity and viability that persist in the present. However well-taken, these explanations do not affect the point that, save perhaps for the self-consciousness with which this and related claims to equality are made by the new states, there is little that is novel about them.

Nor is it only with respect to the state's internal freedom of action that the new egalitarianism follows the old equality. It does so as well with respect to claims made on behalf of the state's external freedom of action. Thus the insistence on the right of self-help is as prominent a feature of the system projected by the new egalitarianism as it was of the traditional system. Nor is the contention relevant here that in the new system self-help will serve the cause of justice, that it will operate to further the independence, development, and "real" equality of those who were so long repressed by the traditional system. Even if the operation of self-help were to promote these ends, and even if recourse to it by the new states were to be regularly supported by voting majorities in the General Assembly, the *structure* of the new system would nevertheless bear an essential resemblance to the old.

Moreover, there is little reason to expect that the scope accorded the exercise of the right of self-help would be significantly narrowed in the new system. At least, there is little reason to expect this unless it is assumed that, among themselves at any rate, the new states will not have the conflicts that states have had in the past, that instead they will manifest an altogether unprecedented solidarity in their mutual relations. But the record to date indicates that the new states may be expected to behave toward one another in much the same way as the older states behaved. For the time being, a measure of solidarity may be manifested by virtue of a common sense of grievance and the expectation that each may benefit through unity against the developed countries. On a broad range of issues that cannot be readily related to the common conflict with the developed world, the behavior of the new states toward one another reveals little novelty. In their territorial disputes, for example, the new states have shown no more disposition to forgo a traditional freedom of action, to relinquish a right of self-help, and to submit to third party judgment than was shown in similar disputes that in an earlier period marked the relations of Western states. India, to take the state that for years was the self-chosen exemplar of the new states, demonstrates a consistent and illuminating record in this respect (though, of course, others do so as well). Moreover, the "legalism" new states often reject in disputes with Western countries, on the ground that the existing law is the product of and reflects the interests of the Western countries, may or may not be rejected in disputes with their own. As a working rule, it will be rejected if opposed to the particular claims of a new state and embraced if consonant with these claims, irrespective of whether or not the dispute is a legacy of the colonial era. All this is commonplace and merely reflects the ubiquitous operation of reason of state, the nerve root of the insistence upon preserving one's freedom of action and leaving broad scope to the exercise of the right of self-help.

This insistence must be all the more apparent, and accentuated, where the interests and demands of states are of a broadly revisionist character. The interests and demands of the new egalitarianism are evidently of such character, directed as they are against a system that has held the new states for so long in subjection and still is alleged to place them at crippling disadvantage. The insistence upon retaining freedom of action is apparent enough even where the parties concerned are more or less satisfied with the status quo. In the new egalitarianism, it is precisely the global status quo of wealth and power reflected by different levels of development that is very much at issue. Quite apart from other reasons, an insistence on the part of the new states with their freedom of action is only to be expected.

The challenge to the global status quo of wealth and power is a challenge by states made on behalf of states. The subjects of the new egalitarianism are states and states alone. It is states and states alone that have duties and, above all, rights. In this respect as well, the new egalitarianism is little more than a refurbished version of the old equality. As such, there is no warrant for seeing in it the necessary precursor of a growing equality within states. The growth of equality among states may prove quite compatible with a continuing, even perhaps a deepening, inequality among individuals within states. Nor will it do to attempt to turn this point aside, or, at the very least, to diminish its significance, by insisting that "after all" states are made up of individuals and, in consequence, a growing equality among states must eventually lead to a growing equality among individuals within states. It may or may not do so. States may develop in a manner that promotes equality or that accentuates inequality. They may emphasize domestic welfare objectives or external power objectives. The new states already afford striking illustrations of the varying consequences that may attend development.

Whatever the meaning we may give to the equality of states, the assumption that the consequences of state equality need not be clearly distinguished from their consequences for individual equality can only lead to confusion and worse. The almost wholly abortive attempts since World War II to secure the effective internationalization of basic civil rights provide a clear illustration of this point. To the extent that the civil rights movement has made any progress—and such progress has been miniscule—it is not unfair to say that it has been made despite the insistent assertion by states of their rights— among which the right of equality has been paramount. The central thrust of the claim to equality in international politics and law remains not only a claim to the equality of states but also a claim that serves today—as in the past—to reaffirm the view of the state as the exclusive guardian of the interests of, and sole dispenser of justice to, the human beings who comprise it. This claim shows few signs of receding today. Certainly, the new egalitarianism in no way challenges it and, if anything, has given it renewed strength.

It has done so by the very manner in which it has defined the inequality that must be redressed. The disparities against which the new states have rebelled are those disparities that are seen to deprive collectives of "real" independence. The new egalitarianism does not direct its attack simply against disparities of wealth and power per se but against a particular form of disparity. It is not the disparity of the strong and the weak, for this is an inequality inherent in the very nature of the state system, but radical disparities in levels of development that give rise to a special kind of inequality. It is the same disparities that, more than anything else, give rise to a sense of humiliation and resentment more potent than the sense of injustice bred by normal disparities of power.

Even if Thucydides is right in saying that justice is possible only between equals (in power), there remains the argument that a special kind of injustice arises between unequals who are also at different stages of economic and social development. To sympathetic Western liberal elites, the unjust inequalities of the international system are to be found in present disparities in living (consumption) standards and, above all, in the extreme poverty endured by almost one-third of the world's people. To the elites of the developing states, whatever their resentment over present disparities in living standards, the essential injustice of the international system is to be found in the very condition of collective backwardness and in the special vulnerabilities felt to result from this condition. The deeper significance of the need for economic development, one perceptive observer writes with pardonable exaggeration, "has few if any economic springs. It arises from a desire to assume full human status by taking part in an industrial civilization, participation in which *alone* enables a nation or an individual to compel others to treat it as an equal." * Similarly, the deeper significance of the new egalitarianism is not to be found in the economic demands it addresses to the developed world—important though these demands undoubtedly are—but in the moral and political roots of these demands. The new egalitarianism expresses above all the desire of the elites of the new states to achieve a collective status that will insure their recognition as equals, even if such recognition initially takes the form of hostility on the part of those defenders of the status quo. Indeed, it may well be that the search for status—for recognition as equals and thus for confirmation of independence—can only be satisfied largely through conflict. Whereas concessions by the developed states may well be seen as but a further confirmation of a persisting inequality, the conflicts marking attempts to drive the hardest possible bargain will confirm, as perhaps nothing else, that sense of equality so evidently sought by the new states.

It is not individual inequality, then, that forms the gravamen of the indictment brought by the new egalitarianism against the present order but collective inequality, and above all the inequality of states at very different stages of development. This point cannot be emphasized too strongly, given the propensity of Western observers to view "global inequality" primarily in terms of individual disparities of income and wealth, thereby implying that in dealing with this issue we are in effect dealing with a familiar issue of domestic justice, though

* Ernest Gellner, "Scale and Nation," *Philosophy of the Social Sciences* 3 (1973): 15, 16. Gellner continues: "Inability to take part in [an industrial civilization] makes a nation militarily powerless against its neighbours, administratively unable to control its own citizens, and culturally incapable of speaking the international language. Pre-industrial man is human, in the modern world, only in a latent sense, by courtesy."

in this instance writ large. Instead, we are dealing primarily with a quite different issue, one that may bear only limited resemblance to the issue of domestic justice. The greater measure of collective equality the new states demand, and may eventually obtain, does not ensure a greater measure of individual equality. In the new egalitarianism, as in the old, states are both the agents and subjects of equality, just as they are the agents and subjects of justice generally. If the claim to a greater measure of collective equality is made in the name of international justice, the domestic purposes to which this equality may be put are nevertheless largely beyond the purview of this justice. And they are so because the state is the moral unit around which claims for equality center, just as it is the moral unit that is held to endow these claims with legitimacy.*

The new egalitarianism challenges not the essential structure of the international system but the distribution of wealth and power within this system. However the system is defined that is held responsible for present global inequalities of wealth and power, it is not the state system per se that is condemned. On the contrary, it is primarily through the institution of the state—and, of course, cooperation among the new states—that the historically oppressed and disadvantaged are to mount a successful challenge to persisting unjust inequalities. Viewed from one perspective, this challenge may seem revolutionary, as indeed it is. Viewed from another and yet more profound perspective, this challenge appears altogether tradi-

---

* The intent of these remarks is not to deny the obvious, that the new egalitarianism has individual as well as collective goals—though the degree to which there is a concern with raising individual living standards, and doing so in a reasonably equitable manner, varies markedly from one developing country to the next. Instead, it is to question the familiar view that "the improvement of the individual lives of the great masses of people is, in the end, what development is all about." Contrary to this statement of Robert McNamara's, this is *not* what development is *all* about as far as the elites of many—indeed most—of the new states are concerned. If it were, Mr. McNamara would not be so concerned with what he deems to be the rising inequities in income distribution patterns within most of the developing countries where disparities in income distribution are considerably greater than in the developed states. The main point at issue is the failure to see the primacy the new egalitarianism regularly places on collective (national) goals and its insistence—with few exceptions—upon subordinating individual to collective goals when the two conflict.

tional. Whatever the view we may take toward the demands the new states have addressed to the industrialized states, in dealing with those demands for greater equality we are standing on familiar terrain. The stage is much larger than it has ever been. There are more actors on it than ever before. Even so, the actors are still states, their conflicts occur in a society that remains dominated by the institution of self-help, and they are contending over goods states have regularly contended over in the past.

VII

An emphasis on the continuity between the old and the new equality, though essential, can be overdone. In some respects, the new egalitarianism is little more than a refurbished version of the old equality, which was quite compatible with almost all forms of inequality; in other respects, the new egalitarianism is indeed new. The powerful are not to employ their power, certainly not their military power, against the weak on behalf of interests whose defense would have evoked the threat or use of force only a short time ago. Intended primarily to deny the legitimacy of armed intervention in response to action a government may take within its territorial jurisdiction, the prohibition has also been extended to cover issues of so-called global management (e.g., conflicting claims over the use and exploitation of the oceans and space). At the same time, the developed states are to acknowledge a duty to assist the underdeveloped states in the great task of reducing the material disparities among them. The prevention of nuclear war apart, this task forms the most important purpose of the new international order. Here again, the Declaration on the Establishment of a New International Economic Order may be cited as representative of the new egalitarianism. The principal purpose of the new order, the declaration reads, is to alter a system wherein the developing countries "which constitute 70 percent of the world population, account for only 30 percent of the world's income." A substantial reduction of inequality in the global distribution of income forms the collective responsibility of the developed states. The framework within which this duty is to be implemented, however, must be one designed by the "whole international community," the collective decisions of the community reflecting the principle of political equality.*

In these respects, the new egalitarianism can scarcely be reconciled with the old equality, which was defined largely in terms of the state's freedom of action. In law, this freedom of action consisted primarily in the recognition by others of an equal claim to the right of self-help. Legal equality formalized the state's independence and, in consequence, its sovereign right of self-help. In turn, the political equality of states provided for in the traditional system formed little more than a corollary of their legal equality. States were deemed politically equal insofar as they could not be bound by agreements or arrangements reached by others to which they had not given their express or tacit consent. At international congresses or conferences to which some or all of the small states might be invited, this meant that in the absence of otherwise agreed upon procedure questions were settled by a majority vote, each state having a right to one vote. But legal equality did not imply an equal capacity for rights, let alone an equality of rights. It was not incompatible with a wide range of formal differentiations in status; still less was it incompatible with

* The duty developed states are to acknowledge is thus rooted in the principle of political equality. Traditionally, of course, this principle created no duty for states. In no way could it be employed to limit the states' freedom of action. If nevertheless the new states see it today as creating a duty, this is because political equality is assimilated to the majoritarian principle, the latter finding its primary expression in the United Nations General Assembly. And since the majority is made up of the Southern states, in practice the operation of this principle has been to limit—more accurately, perhaps, to harass—the North. In fact, the new states have not consistently adhered to any one formula through which to express the majority principle. Indeed, the very meaning of "majority" has varied, depending upon the context in which it is invoked. On strictly political issues, the majority has been generally considered in terms of states and, in consequence, expressed by the "one state, one vote" formula. On economic issues, however, the meaning of "majority"—as the quotation in the text indicates—has often been considered in terms of percentages of world population represented by the developed and developing states. Democratization of economic institutions is, in theory at least, designed to roughly reflect population percentages.

66

striking substantive inequalities. Nor did political equality imply anything even approximating an equality of capacity to participate in, let alone to affect, the political process. It was satisfied, when observed, by the formality of representation.

Given the disparities of wealth and power among states, the old equality was compatible not only with almost any and all degrees of substantive inequality but also with a *de facto*—and often a *de jure*—denial of equality of opportunity.* In part, this denial simply resulted from the very disparities of wealth and power that characterized the international system. In part, this denial also resulted, paradoxically, from an equality defined in terms of an equal claim to the right of self-help. For the freedom of action sanctioned by the traditional right of self-help largely precluded the emergence of conditions in which equality of opportunity could prove meaningful.

Although the new egalitarianism follows the old equality in making the state's sovereign independence the centerpiece of the new order, it does not accept the consequences that have heretofore attended the state's claim to sovereign independence. It does not accept these consequences just as it is no longer content with the legal and political equality that were the formal expressions of the state's independence. Equality is still synonymous with independence, but independence is itself given a new dimension in that it is seen to encompass and, indeed, to require the equal opportunity of states—above all, the disadvantaged states—to develop their potential. The potential for development, it is argued, cannot be secured by confining equality to its legal and political forms, even if these forms were given expanded significance. It can only be secured by extending an ever increasing equality of opportunity to the economic level.

Yet it is this extension that has been denied by the beneficiaries of the present international system, despite what the new states deem the essential injustice of the pattern of relationships on which this system has always rested. The crux of the indictment the new states have brought against the present system deals not only with the insti-

* We are defining equality of opportunity here in terms of equal capacity to participate in the competitive process.

tutionalized disparity of benefits this order confers as between the developed and underdeveloped countries; it also deals with the way in which these disparities were created and the manner in which they are sustained even today. A colonial past, based upon force, gave rise to present disparities. A neo-colonialism, even when no longer based upon force, perpetuates these disparities by virtue of the advantages conferred by an unjust history. The laws of the market insure that between states unequal in economic power and at very different stages of development there can only be further inequality. The post-World War II institutions that apotheosized the principles of a liberal international economy, and that were created without the participation of the new states and without consideration for their interests, must accordingly be replaced by a new order that is, when necessary, as discriminating in favor of the underdeveloped states as the present order is discriminating in favor of the industrial countries. As between unequals, the new egalitarianism insists, any order that finds primary expression in the principle of equality of opportunity, yet in doing so fails to discriminate in favor of the disadvantaged, is itself discriminatory and unjust.

It is largely on this basis that one may understand the insistence of the developing countries that *every* state, by virtue of its sovereign equality, has exclusive control over its own resources and that *some* states have a duty to share their resources with others. Provided that one accepts the argument justifying discriminatory treatment in favor of the materially disadvantaged, there is no difficulty in reconciling these apparently contradictory claims. Julius Stone has expressed the view that in their insistence upon exclusive control over the use and disposition of their own resources the new states have "constructed needless barriers to some of their central needs for the future, namely the acceptance by more affluent states of some level of duty to transfer resources to other states to meet the direst material needs of great sections of mankind." * But supposedly "needless barriers" might be removed here only by the concession of a claim responding to anxieties that are the result of a long history of domination and for-

---

* Julius Stone, *Of Law and Nations* (Buffalo: Wm. S. Hein, 1974), p. 361.

mal inequality. Rather than make such a concession, the new states insist upon a double standard of behavior. In turn, this standard is partially justified by invoking a past in which material disparities presumably arose because of what is seen as a double standard imposed on developing peoples. Whether explicitly or, as is more often the case, implicitly, the demand for discriminatory treatment is based in some measure on a repressive and exploited past.* Even in the absence of that past, the institutional imbalances of the present system would not be justified. The indictment of the contemporary order can stand on its own, as the proponents of a new order are at pains to insist. Still, it is apparent that to the extent the force of this indictment depends upon a sense of grievance of those pressing it, and upon a sense of moral unease of those to whom it is made, the invocation of an unjust past is of more than merely marginal significance.

Whether it is the past or the present that is invoked, the thrust of the new egalitarianism is to require intervention on behalf of the materially disadvantaged, since without such intervention there can be no equality of opportunity. The institutional reforms demanded in the trade infrastructure and in the monetary system, the new mechanisms proposed for the transfer of greater resources from the developed to the underdeveloped countries, and the insistence upon an increased role of the developing states in all international economic institutions are designed to secure equality of opportunity. But the equality of opportunity asked for is not the equality of treatment that is identified by the developed capitalist nations with the free market system and that is the economic expression of the principle of self-help. For the latter turns out to be the perversion of true equality of opportunity. In a society of approximate equals, this would not be so. In a society marked instead by radical inequalities, equality of treatment can only lead to discrimination in favor of the stronger.†

---

* That past, however, is not to be associated necessarily with colonization but with the operation of the free market.

† In this respect, the new egalitarianism will be recognized as following very closely a classic liberal argument. Although the latter endorsed the principle of self-help as defining, to all intents and purposes, a free market, it also assumed a society of approximate equals in opportunity and, indeed, in power.

This condemnation of the market in the new egalitarianism is, and can be, no more than qualified and provisional. Given the diversity of socio-economic systems entertained by the developing states, a more sweeping condemnation would prove divisive, since many of the states are evidently not opposed in principle to a free market economy. What they all are opposed to, though even here in varying degree, is the manner in which the market operates internationally among separate economies at very different levels of development. There is no evidence that this opposition would persist—the socialist states *possibly* apart—once these disparities were markedly narrowed. Besides, it is not easy to see how this opposition can be maintained as a matter of principle as long as the essential structure of the state system is endorsed. If the free market is the economic expression of the principle of self-help, the global system of exchange it necessitates can scarcely disappear before the state system itself disappears.* In sum, it is not the market system as such that the new egalitarianism sets its face against but the "unfair"—because unequal—conditions in which the developing states are compelled to participate in this system.

Nor is this all. The discrimination that is presumably required if equality of opportunity is to be achieved cannot be considered apart from the need to achieve greater equality of condition.† Occasionally, this point has been obscured—intentionally or unintentionally—by the spokesmen of the new egalitarianism who are only too aware of Western sensitivity to demands for a significant redistribution of *existing* wealth. Even if the demand is for future rather

---

* The substitute for the free market system would be a "distributor" in the Aristotelian sense—in our terms, a world state.

† "The so-called laws of supply and demand," the Algerian foreign minister Adelaziz Bouteflika declared to the U.N. General Assembly 7th Special Session on Development and International Economic Cooperation (Sept. 2, 1975), "in reality merely reflect an imposed relationship, based on the respective strengths of the seller and buyer. . . . In fact, the only approach which will bring about the most equitable situation will inevitably involve the redistribution of income. Otherwise, the laws of the market, dominated as it is by the strongest and most resilient, will continue to fuel the deterioration in the terms of trade of the developing countries in an implacable process which enriches the richest while impoverishing the poorest."

than existing global wealth the share of future wealth that is demanded is markedly greater than the present share. It is only by increasing the developing states' share of future global wealth that present disparities can be progressively narrowed. We are not dealing here with the prospect of a larger cake the pieces of which are to remain proportionately the same for all parties, but with a larger cake in which the pieces that will go to some parties (the developing countries) are to become proportionately larger. A new distribution of future global wealth is called for, in part to achieve greater equality of opportunity and in part to achieve greater equality of condition. The prospects of growth entertained by the new egalitarianism must be distinguished, then, from the prospects of growth entertained within Western societies, where growth is still expected to yield (as it has yielded in the past) only proportionately larger returns to all parties.

It is in the light of these considerations that we may read a recent statement by protagonists of a new international economic order that declares: ". . . we wish to make it clear that the Third World is not demanding a massive redistribution of the wealth of the rich nations. Nor is it seeking equality of income. It is asking for equality of opportunity." * Yet the "loss" of economic opportunities the Third World is alleged to suffer as a result of institutional distortions is calculated to be of such proportions that if recovered would lead to substantially greater equality of condition. The relationship of equality of opportunity to greater equality of condition is not simply one of cause and effect, though it is of course that as well. In part, it is also considered as precisely the reverse relationship, since without a greater equality of condition, the argument runs, equality of opportunity will prove to be at best a precarious achievement.

This is the burden of nearly every pronouncement the new states and their elites have made over the past decade, and however excessive the rhetoric in which these expressions have been cast there is no question that they express accurately enough a shared sense of injustice. This sense of injustice has not been alleviated by a legal and po-

---

* *Proposals for a New International Economic Order* (Report to the Third World Forum at Mexico City, August 21–24, 1975), p. 3.

litical equality that is seen as deprived largely of substantive significance in the absence of a greater measure of economic equality. In fact, recent experience has shown that even in international society legal and, particularly, political equality may have more than a merely formal significance. To the degree that the "one state, one vote" rule is given expanded scope and application, it gives the weak a role in shaping—or reshaping—the order of international society they did not formerly possess, in that it imposes upon the powerful the need to obtain legitimation of their interests—or, at least, some of their interests—through international forums in which the consent of majorities is accepted procedure. Novel constraints are thereby placed on great states, requiring them to bargain with small states in a manner they would not have deigned in the past.

At the same time, it is true that while the aspects of international relations presently requiring multilateral regulation, and thus potentially vulnerable to the "one state, one vote" rule, are increasing, there remain many vital areas of state life that are unaffected by the operation of political equality. Even in many areas clearly requiring multilateral regulation there is little, if any, prospect that this potential vulnerability will be realized. The "democratization" of existing international institutions is a formula the developing states have employed to demand a greater voting strength for the Third World as a bloc. In demanding that this voting strength should be roughly equal to that of the industrialized nations, the appeal is not only to a principle of political equality. Behind that appeal is also the recognition of a collective power to disrupt if a greater measure of equality is not granted. Besides, unless we assume that operation of this rule in international society will come to play at least as great a role as it does in domestic societies—clearly an absurd assumption—its ultimate impact on the reduction of disparities of income and wealth must be reckoned as very modest.

III

Equality and Order

I

THE ORDER of the new egalitarianism is an order of states par excellence. The principle of sovereign equality is the foundation of the new system. The justice of the new egalitarianism is, first and foremost, a collective justice. In these respects, the new egalitarianism plainly resembles the old equality. Yet it is expected to yield results quite different from the results that attended the old equality. Although the new system will remain one dominated by self-help, it will no longer function to preserve the inequalities of the past. The strong will no longer exact what they can and the weak grant what they must. Instead, the weak will increasingly acquire the means to resist the depredations of the strong and to redress age-old imbalances.

How is this to be done? How is it possible to retain the essential structure of the state system while not only escaping but indeed reversing the consequences to which this system has regularly led? What will induce the rich and powerful in international society to yield, if only in part, what has only so recently and often so reluctantly been yielded in domestic society? "A new distribution of wealth will not take place spontaneously," the Iraqi delegate declared to the 1975 General Assembly Session on Development and International Economic Cooperation, "anymore than it will happen in the name of justice or by means of mere dialogue." The same may be said for the process by which a new distribution of power will take place. Will such distribution take place, however, as a result of a growing awareness on the part of the developed and capitalist states that they are vulnerable to the disruptive courses of action open to the developing states?

The theme of the vulnerability of the developed states to the disruptive behavior of the developing countries, and particularly if the latter are united, is given constant expression by the spokesmen of the new egalitarianism. The economy of the West, in the words of the Algerian foreign minister, "imposing though it be, rests on fragile and vulnerable foundations." It does so if only by virtue of the developed states' dependence on the raw materials of the developing countries. This dependence alone is seen by the elites of the new states as an Archimedean point on which an unequal and unjust world will eventually be moved. It will be moved not simply by the prospect of more producer cartels. This prospect is not in fact threatened by the developing states as much as it is demanded as a matter of right in the absence of "just" prices for their principal exports. Instead, what is threatened, rather than promised, is the denial of indispensable commodities to the developed states should the latter prove recalcitrant to the demands of the developing countries.

At the same time, the dependence of the developing on the developed states is not denied. An emphasis on the need of individual and collective self-reliance cannot obscure the reality of a dependence that may only be broken by the developing countries at the risk of jeopardizing their own growth prospects. This risk, indeed, must loom far larger for the better off among the states of the Third World than it does for the truly destitute. Why, then, the insistence that mutual dependence must operate, on balance, to secure the ends of the new egalitarianism? In the main, the answer must be that the relationship of interdependence is not strictly mutual, that in the balance of dependencies it is the developed states' dependencies that are greater than those of the developing states. They are greater for the developed states not so much because these states have more to lose through conflict than do the developing states (after all, being rich, the developed states can afford to lose more) but because they are presumably less willing to lose what a full-scale confrontation might entail. In such confrontation, the developed states run the risk of sacrificing the prospects for future growth. This sacrifice would not be borne passively by publics and by governments that have for so long enjoyed growth and that, in consequence, have come to take it almost for granted. Instead, the cessation of growth would give rise to serious social and political instability in the developed and capitalist countries. Moreover, it would provoke serious conflicts of interest between these countries as each sought to insure access to needed raw materials, though in circumstances characterized by pervasive uncertainty and intense competition. In these circumstances, whatever might remain of the solidarity of the rich would dissolve. At best, the present international system would give way to regional blocs, dominated by the drive to achieve relative self-sufficiency and uneasily juxtaposed with one another. At worst, the restraints characterizing the present system would give way to open rivalry among the developed states as each struggled to prevent its exclusion from resources and markets. As compared with the costs entailed by these prospects, the costs of accommodation to the demands of the developing states are calculated to be quite marginal.

Thus it is not so much the relative costs to each side that are seen as decisive in a deepening conflict between the developed and developing countries, but the ability and willingness of the respective sides to bear the costs. Although the developing countries would clearly suffer, they are expected to bear with far greater equanimity than the developed states the privation that serious conflict might impose upon them. They are expected to do so if for no other reason than that many of them remain very poor, and are therefore accustomed to privation, or have only recently improved their lot. In either case, the capacity to endure privation is considered as much higher than in the developed states of the West.* Then, too, the developing

---

* This is a view that is also shared by many in the West. How else are we to understand the words of the chancellor (then finance minister) of the Federal Republic of Germany: "If it can be assumed that most of the developed countries with a high level of prosperity have a great preference for peace, and that most of the less-developed

countries would be contending for the right to be treated as equals, and for this reason they will be ready to endure considerable sacrifice. In contrast, the denial of equality, and of justice, even if it does not prove morally debilitating to the West, can scarcely be expected to provide the unity and determination required to deal effectively in a protracted struggle with the developing world. A distinguished African intellectual elaborates this theme of the divisive and debilitating effects of wealth (and, conversely, the potentially unifying effects of poverty) in these words:

> Wealth is competitive in a way in which poverty is not. There is a certain level of poverty below which economic competition is minimal and the potential for economic hostility between one poor man and another is really marginal. . . . By the very nature of wealth and of the complexity of trade, rich countries have more potential areas of disagreement in the economic field than poor countries. And the economic troubles of one rich country are more likely to benefit a rival rich country, than the poverty of a poor man can conceivably benefit another.*

In the last analysis, however, the appeal to the self-interest of the developed world is almost invariably cast in terms of unspecified, though dire, consequences if the demands of the new egalitarianism are denied. The vagueness of the threat the future holds for those who insist upon maintaining the status quo is apparent in the following, and representative, statement:

> Historically, the rich have always underestimated the political bargaining power of the poor just because their economic clout is so limited. We would urge the industrialized nations not to make such a mistake. Ultimately, the real bargaining power of the poor is their ability to disrupt the life styles of the rich, whether through a wholesale confrontation or through limited unilateral actions. The rich can never afford to drive the poor to their ultimate

---

countries have a high preference for increased wealth, there must be a level on which a convergence of preferences would stabilize the international political situation at a higher level of prosperity for both the wealthier and currently poorer countries'' (Helmut Schmidt, "The Struggle for the World Product," *Foreign Affairs* 52 [April 1974]: 451).

* Ali A. Mazrui, "The Political Economy of World Order: Modernization and Reform in Africa," in Jagdish N. Bhagwati, ed., *Economic and World Order: From the 1970's to the 1990's* (New York: Macmillan, 1972), p. 290.

despair and belligerence. The avenues of disruption are many: the costs of disruption can be heavy.*

What are we to make of this and countless similar statements? Of what does this "poor power" consist that can disrupt the life styles of the rich, even if the poor fail to unite their forces? History teaches that the poor, because they are poor, rarely pose a serious threat to the custodians and beneficiaries of the status quo, that such threat is posed instead by those who, though far from destitute, have been given just enough that they have the power and will successfully to insist upon more. In the present case, this would mean that the states of the developing world with the ability to disrupt the life styles of the rich are states that may withhold vital commodities from the developed world. But these states are not among the very poor of the Third World. They are, for the most part, among the emerging class, if not the nouveaux riches, of international society. Their power depends not only upon their possession of vital resources (most notably, of course, oil) but also upon the inability or the forebearance of the developed states to take, or even seriously to threaten, severe sanctions against them in the event of exorbitant demands on their part. It is not easy to see the circumstances in which these states would be driven to "ultimate despair and belligerence," though it is quite easy to see the circumstances in which they would continue to make still greater demands on the developed and capitalist countries.

Will past experience nevertheless prove to be a misleading guide to the future? Will the "political bargaining power" of the very poor—roughly a fourth of the world's peoples—consist in the prospect that governments, presiding over inert and despairing masses, will be driven to desperate measures in the hope, however, irrational, that such measures may prompt an otherwise indifferent and callous world to relieve their plight? There is no need to speculate here on the nature of these measures, and somber warnings of the kind cited above rarely do so. It is clear, however, that the "ultimate

* The Third World Forum, *Proposals for a New International Economic Order* (Report given at Mexico City, August 21, 24, 1975), p. 15.

despair'' the rich nations are warned against is an allusion to behavior that directly threatens the stability of the international system. Yesterday the world's poor could be left to their own devices with the reasonable assurance that, whatever their suffering, the rich would remain unaffected. Today this assurance can no longer be given, though why it cannot remains unexplained.

I I

The above view of the self-interest the developed states presumably have in reaching accommodation with the new egalitarianism has not met with general resistance among Western liberal elites. If anything, it forms a mirror image, in many respects, of arguments that have become commonplace in the West. In at least one critical respect, the Western reaction has given still greater persuasiveness to the considerations of self-interest invoked by the new states. It has done so by placing these considerations in the context of an international system in which the role of military power is found to have undergone a very marked change. Although still a system dominated by self-help, the utility of what was traditionally the decisive form of self-help has been profoundly altered, it is urged, and perhaps irrevocably so. The implications of this change for the challenge to inequality appear to follow ineluctably.

Clearly, if the inequalities that have traditionally marked state relations are to decline, the institution that has afforded the primary means for maintaining inequality must also decline. The effective challenge to inequality requires, at the outset, that the more extreme forms of self-help—especially military force—no longer perform their time-honored functions. Provided that physical coercion of the weak by the strong has largely lost its former utility, as many now believe, nothing would appear to be of comparable moment in altering the hierarchical structure of international society. Given the nature of this society, the essential precondition for almost any meaningful version of equality—legal, political, or economic—is the emergence of effective restraints on the state's traditional license to resort to armed force. It is in the assumption that the rising material and moral costs of employing force now effectively inhibit—or very nearly so—the strong from resorting to force against the weak that we must find one of the root sources, if not *the* root source, of the challenge to inequality.

Nor is it reasonable to expect that a growing disutility of military power will have no effect on the economic power wielded by the strong. Although radical disparities in economic power remain in a world where military power is presumed to be increasingly at a discount, the effects of these disparities must surely be altered as well, and in the same direction. Power may not be indivisible, but the burden of proof is on those who would argue that, though the utility of military power has markedly declined, there need be no devaluation in the efficacy of economic power. Curiously, it is precisely the opposite conclusion that is drawn—or simply assumed—by most observers today. For the prevailing view finds the decline in the utility of military power largely compensated by the rise in the utility of economic power.* In this view "power" remains, as it were, a con-

---

* This is the view taken, for example, by C. Fred Bergsten, Robert O. Keohane, and Joseph S. Nye, Jr. in their recent essay, "International Economics and International Politics: A Framework for Analysis," in C. Fred Bergsten and Lawrence B. Krause, eds., *World Politics and International Economics* (Washington: The Brookings Institution, 1975), pp. 6–10. Instances cited where "economic sources of power allow governments to carry on 'war by other means' " are: the Allied blockade against Napoleon, the League of Nations oil embargo against Italy, the U.S. embargo of exports to Cuba, the United Nations sanctions against Rhodesia, and the embargo of oil sales to the United States and the Netherlands by Arab states in 1973–74 in pursuit of a favorable political settlement in the Middle East. In fact, these instances merely serve to underline the contrary argument made above. The Allied blockade against Napoleon was part and parcel of a military struggle and is meaningful only within that context. The League of Nations so-called oil embargo against Italy was a failure because, among other reasons, Britain and France would not contemplate military sanctions. The U.S. embargo of exports to Cuba provides a striking illustration of the limits of economic coercion alone. The same must be said of the U.N. sanctions against Rhodesia. The Arab 1973–74 oil embargo (and perhaps the threat of another embargo) is at least a debatable instance of economic power allowing governments to carry on "war by other means." However, even this example is suspect. The embargo was not pressed seriously because the Arab states could not press it beyond very modest limits without risking a military response.

stant. Hence the decline in one form of power (military) must be expected to result in the rise of another form (economic). Is this doctrine of the "substitutability" of power valid, or even approximately so? One must seriously doubt that it is. Certainly, economic power is significant and perhaps decisive over a considerable range of issues. but the most casual examination will show that these are largely the issues over which economic power has traditionally played a central role. Typically, they are issues that states do not relate—or do not directly relate—to their security and independence, whether understood in the narrow or broad sense. The critical question, though, is whether economic power can play the role, if only approximately, played in the past by military power. Can it determine issues that relate to the state's security and independence, or, for that matter, its status? It will not do to respond to this question by pointing once again to the decline in the utility of military power, even over issues that involve the state's security in the greater-than-physical sense. Although it may be true that military power has so declined, it does not follow that economic power has accordingly risen.* Instead, it may be that power itself is increasingly at a discount and what military power can no longer do economic power also can no longer do. Thus to the degree that in conflict situations involving "vital interests" economic power has been the handmaiden of military power, the decline of the latter will simply signal the decline of the former.

Indeed, recent experience has shown that even against a very small state, and one with a vulnerable economy, the effectiveness of economic coercion alone may prove surprisingly limited. In part, this is so for the evident reason that economic coercion permits the weak alternatives that physical coercion does not. Then, too, the limited effectiveness of economic coercion may in some measure be attributed to the same sources that limit the effectiveness of physical coercion. Although the legitimacy of the former had not been subject

---

* At least, it does not follow unless one assumes a very broad and pervasive consensus in international society that permits economic power to substitute, in large measure, for military power. But there is no evidence that such consensus exists today, despite the growing belief to the contrary.

to the same standards as has the latter, economic coercion has been called increasingly into question even when employed by a wealthy country to protect interests that are the result of undertakings a weaker (underdeveloped) state consented to.* This argument draws added force once it is recognized that economic coercion can only be fully effective to the extent that it leaves open the option of physical coercion. In this respect, it is quite understandable that many who rejected serious economic confrontation in the oil crisis did so in part on the ground that this could lead eventually to military confrontation. Finally, in the case of economic coercion—as in the case of physical coercion—the same argument will be, and has been, employed: the costs may well outweigh the gains, whether economic or political, in a world where the poor and weak have displayed increasing sensitivity to any form of coercion. It is particularly for the latter reason that one observer concludes: "The value of economic threats seems, at present at least, subject to secular depreciation." †

The erosion of military and, in some measure at least, economic power as instruments of the strong must clearly have, if continued, a profound impact on the hierarchical nature of international society and, in turn, the very character of international order. Even so, this erosion cannot of itself confer the kind of leverage needed to effect a significant redistribution of the world's wealth. The reduction of material disparities among states is affected by the new constraints on force largely to the extent that these constraints permit the weak to

---

* It serves no useful purpose here to enter into extended discussion of what constitutes "consent" as between parties greatly unequal in power. If the fact of inequality per se is held to invalidate the consensual nature of an undertaking, then almost any bilateral agreement between developed and underdeveloped countries may be regarded as invalid. An apparently more plausible attack on the validity of agreements entered into between the rich and the poor holds that the test must turn on exploitation rather than inequality per se. In fact, the alternative turns out to reveal almost as many difficulties as the test it replaces. Cf. pp. 117–26.

† Klaus Knorr, *Power and Wealth: The Political Economy of International Power* (New York: Basic Books, 1973), p. 197. Elsewhere Knorr writes: "As long . . . as international economic and political competition makes the monopolist and monopsonist market power of some states over others very precarious and subject to swift dissipation, and as long as pressured governments are resolute and domestically strong, the prospects for economic warriors are bound to be dim."

take measures within their territories that in an earlier day would have invited armed intervention. In this sense, a restricted scope afforded to forcible measures of self-help may diminish—and for one select group of countries spectacularly so—disparities in wealth. Yet it is only in this sense that the new constraints may do so. In consequence, their effects—again, the case of oil apart—would appear to be rather peripheral in reducing material disparities.

In a broader perspective, however, the leverage Third World states are expected to enjoy by virtue of their possession of natural resources indispensable to the industrialized states is only one feature of a more general vision in which the vulnerabilities of the strong will become increasingly apparent. The dependence of the rich on the raw materials held by the poor is only the most recent and dramatic manifestation of this vision. The vision would persist in the absence of concern over the continued supply of raw materials at less than exorbitant prices. It is to be found in the repeated admonition that we cannot begin to solve the many environmental problems we face without the cooperation of the Third World states. It is also to be found in a host of economic issues other than natural resources—investments, markets, monetary reform, trade liberalization—in which the Third World is considered to have the power to "hold us up." *

Still, it is not these and related issues that form the crux of the conviction that present inequalities of nations—above all, material inequalities—must somehow be reduced. Instead, the essence of the challenge to inequality is the presumed danger that these inequalities pose to international peace and stability. The power of the weak that is most to be feared, in this view, is the power to transmit misery in the form of chaos and war. The power to transmit misery might take a passive form in the sense that it would provide the occasion for conflicts ultimately involving the rich and strong.† In this sense, the

---

* Cf. C. Fred Bergsten, "The Threat Is Real," *Foreign Policy* 14 (Spring 1974): 84 ff.

† The passive ability to transmit misery is what Inis Claude terms "the notion of passive provocation." This he defines as "the danger . . . not that states of marginal viability will start a fight, but that they will be fought over—not that they are probable aggressors, but that they are potential objects of rivalry and arenas for intervention and

power of the very poor and only marginally viable states is the power such states have often possessed in the past. In a competitive system of self-help, these states form a magnet for great-power rivalry. The difference between yesterday and today, though, is that the prospective magnets are quite numerous and the temptations (or compulsions) they hold out to great powers threaten consequences that may prove more destructive than ever.

Alternatively, the power to transmit misery might well take, in the view of some, an active form. Thus there is the scenario of a world in which the governments of poor states, at once increasingly revolutionary in outlook yet unable to raise the living standards of their ever burgeoning populations, will threaten desperate measures against the rich nations in order to compel the latter to undertake a massive transfer of wealth to the world's poor. What is seen to give apparent plausibility to an otherwise fanciful projection of a future in which the poor may threaten the rich is the prospect that nuclear weapons will become increasingly available, even to states whose economies otherwise remain at an undeveloped stage. The possession of a very modest number of nuclear weapons, together with some means—however simple and improvised—of delivering them, might then be used by the poor as a means to coerce the rich into undertaking such transfers of wealth that experience indicates would not otherwise be seriously considered.

But whether this transmission of misery takes an active or a passive form is held to be less important than the vulnerability of the rich to whatever form it takes. We have become familiar with the metaphors that are intended to convey this sense of the vulnerability of the world's favored peoples to conditions that may one day prompt the less fortunate and their governments to desperate behavior. The United States, Samuel Huntington writes, "is a tenant oc-

---

counter-intervention. Such states endanger the peace not by their policy but by their predicament, not by posing threats but by presenting temptations to outside powers to compete for the privilege of filling the power vacuums they represent" (Inis L. Claude, "Economic Development Aid and International Political Stability," in Robert W. Cox, ed., *The Politics of International Organizations* [New York: Praeger, 1970], p. 55).

cupying the largest, most elegant, most luxuriously furnished penthouse suite in a global apartment house.'' As such, we have ''a clear interest in insuring that the structure as a whole is sound and that minimum conditions for decent human existence prevail in the building.'' * Robert L. Heilbroner puts the matter more generally, as well as more ominously, in these terms: ''Even the most corrupt governments of the underdeveloped world are aware of the ghastly resemblance of the world's present economic conditions to an immense train, in which a few passengers, mainly in the advanced capitalist world, ride in first-class coaches, in conditions of comfort unimaginable to the enormously greater numbers crammed into the cattle cars that make up the bulk of the train's carriages.'' † Eventually, in the absence of a greater equality, the world's apartment house or train will be subject to dangers that may threaten all the inhabitants or passengers. But it is the rich among them who are presumably the more vulnerable, if only for the reason that they have a great deal to lose.

Thus in what almost appears as a reversal of the ''natural'' order of things, it is the weak of the world who are considered to pose grave peril to the strong. Moral obligation apart, it is the world's interdependence—indeed, its indivisibility—that compels us out of self-interest to reduce present material disparities between the world's rich and poor. The appeal to self-interest resulting from an inescapable interdependence need not and should not be understood only in the narrow sense of avoiding material injury. Even if the poor could be safely left to their suffering, the prospect of living in a prosperous enclave that is surrounded by a despairing world would prove unwelcome. More than that, it is argued, this prospect must eventually prove morally debilitating, especially given our awareness today of conditions from which it was once possible and rather easy to divert our attention.‡

* Samuel P. Huntington, ''Foreign Aid: For What and For Whom,'' *Foreign Policy* 2 (Spring 1971): 130–31.

† Heilbroner, *Inquiry Into the Human Prospect,* p. 39.

‡ Robert A. Packenham articulates our ''moral interest'' in Third World development in these terms: ''It is very much in the interest of the United States to maintain and revitalize its moral consciousness. A nation that is in moral decay can decline just

Equality and Order

It is in this manner that a view initially based upon calculations of self-interest moves almost imperceptibly to one based upon moral obligation. The prospect of moral debilitation is still an appeal to self-interest. That appeal must fail if it cannot be established that ignoring the world's poor will prove morally debilitating. Moral obligation, on the other hand, remains unaffected by such demonstration. Our duty to reduce the material disparities between the world's rich and poor does not depend upon whether our act of sharing contributes to our moral betterment. Still less does this duty depend upon whether its fulfillment enables us to avoid the consequences that are presumably attendant upon poverty and desperation. In arguing that the reduction of material disparities must be motivated "by human solidarity with, and compassion for, the needy," Gunnar Myrdal scornfully rejects "the glib assertion that the underdeveloped countries must be aided in order to preserve peace in the world." On the contrary, our duty to aid the poor holds even though "if any generalization can be made, it is rather that people become restless and rebellious when they are getting a little better off, but not enough so." * Similarly, our duty to aid the poor holds, in this view, even though it may prove insignificant as a contribution to collective moral regeneration.

If the standard of disinterestedness Myrdal sets as the proper motivation for helping the world's poor is too austere for most, a more diluted form of obligation is nevertheless apparent in the view that present disparities between rich and poor must be substantially reduced. The sentiment of sympathy or pity may not appear in unalloyed form, but it is clearly there even though combined with anxiety over the actions to which the poor may finally be driven in the attempt to alter their condition. Since the same combination was

---

as surely as—though more subtly than—a nation with deficient material defenses. It seems dubious that the United States can maintain its moral sensitivity, and live up to its ideals, if it ignores the poverty of poor nations. We are . . . an island of affluence in a sea of poverty. Even if this situation posed no security threat, it would pose a moral threat—indeed, it already does" (*Liberal America and the Third World* [Princeton: Princeton Univ. Press, 1973], pp. 327–28).

* Gunnar Myrdal, "The World Poverty Problem," Britannica Book of the Year, 1972 (Chicago: *Encyclopedia Britannica,* 1972), p. 34.

once a commonplace in arguments for greater equality within Western societies, it is not surprising that it should form the basis for appeals to reduce inequalities in international society. What is surprising is the rather casual manner with which a collective moral responsibility that encompasses humanity is increasingly viewed as almost self-evident.

III

What are we to make of these scenarios of a world in which the rich and powerful * will yield, if only out of self-interest, what they have never yielded in the past? Are they persuasive or even plausible? Certainly, reasons are not lacking for treating them with skepticism.

---

* Many will doubtless take exception to the coupling in these pages of the "rich" and the "powerful," particularly those who do not share the view—as I do not—that economic power can take the place of military power in a period when the utility of military power is held to have decline markedly. The distinction between rich states and powerful states arises not only in the present period. It goes back at least to Machiavelli, who asked whether it was better to have gold or to have arms (and who answered, not unexpectedly, that it was better to have arms, since with the latter one could always take gold from those without arms). In fact, those who have had gold (wealth) have almost always had arms as well. Save for quite small states, the rich have also been the powerful. And if not the *actually* (or immediately) powerful then the *potentially* powerful, since wealth could be translated into military power, given the necessary time. In the industrial age, this relationship between wealth and power has been particularly apparent. The indices of industrial production have been the indices of military power, with two major exceptions: population and, for want of a better term, will. This continues to be the case in the present period. It is obviously so if one takes the view that economic power must largely fill the void left by the declining utility of military power. But even if this view is rejected, the rich remain the powerful unless they suffer from utter absence of will to convert their wealth into military power, if and when necessary. Whether this utter absence of will characterizes Western Europe and Japan, whether they will remain resistant to acquiring military power other than for the purposes of deterrence and defense, remains an open question. Certainly, both West Germany and Japan have the means to become, once again, militarily powerful states. In the case of Japan, it is clear that the very prospect of rapid rearmament, given the incentive, has had a deterrent effect on the action of Japan's major neighbors. Until the evidence is much stronger that Western Europe and Japan are irrevocably committed, or very nearly so, to being "civilian" powers, I see no persuasive reasons for abandoning the equation made above.

Equality and Order

One apparent reason for skepticism is the potential for conflict among the developing states. That the interests of these states will in time become divergent is only to be expected. Indeed, it is already clear that in many respects the interests of the developing states have become divergent. What nevertheless maintains a residual unity among them is, apart from a shared past, the conviction that they have more to gain at present through suppressing such differences as may be exploited by the developed states.

There is no assurance, though, that this common stake in the emergence of a new order will continue to be perceived as outweighing divergent interests that are already the source of grievance among the developing states. In this respect, although the experience to date with OPEC appears to bear out the strength of the commitment by the developing countries to a united front against the developed world, it also suggests the limits of this commitment. "If what you want is to have all the under-developed countries make the oil battle their own," Fidel Castro has warned the oil cartel, "it is essential for the oil producing countries to make the battle of the under-developed world theirs." But the oil-producing countries can be expected to make the battle of the underdeveloped world theirs only for as long as, and only to the extent that, they need this world. The "new order" need not come to either all or none, as the nouveaux riches among OPEC undoubtedly appreciate. It may come only to some. Once accepted into the new order—or, perhaps more to the point, admitted into the old order—why should the new arrivals continue to identify with those they have left behind? The belief that they will do so may prove to be no more than romanticism, akin to the belief that the poor will necessarily demonstrate more unity and determination in conflict than the rich. They may do so and, if the experience to date with OPEC is an accurate indication of what the future holds, they are likely to do so. A much broader experience indicates, though, that the developing countries are surely no less capable of divisiveness and mutual betrayal than the developed.*

* The strongest case for the view that Southern solidarity will probably not withstand the centrifugal forces arising within the coming years has been made by Roger

The divisive potential of the developing states cannot but cast doubt on the sources of their presumed power. It does so in nearly every respect, though most apparently with respect to the leverage to be gained from the possession of vital raw materials. For that leverage will largely depend upon the ability to fashion and to maintain effective cartels. In the absence of the favorable circumstances attending the oil cartel, however, the maintenance of effective cartels over other commodities may require an extraordinary degree of cohesiveness and a willingness to make at least considerable short-term sacrifices for the common good. Yet even if the developing states meet these requirements, uncertainty persists over the leverage to be gained through cartels other than oil. In part, this is so because the significance of oil far outweighs any other raw material and, it has been argued, all other raw materials that lend themselves to cartelization. In part, this is so because of continuing uncertainty and controversy over the extent to which new sources may be exploited or technology can fashion substitutes to replace many of the raw materials the developed world has heretofore drawn from the developing world. It may still turn out that in this respect the Western states and Japan will prove far less vulnerable to pressure from the Southern states than is currently thought to be the case.

To these uncertainties must be added the further uncertainty attending the estimate commonly drawn today of the declining utility of military power and, what is taken as the corollary of this decline, the growing vulnerability of Western societies to the disruptive behavior of the world's poor. Even if the utility of military power has markedly declined, and even if this decline is seen as irreversible, it does not follow that Western societies are thereby rendered dangerously vulnerable to the disruptive behavior of the world's poor. At least, this does not follow unless it is assumed that the decline in the utility of military power operates not only to forestall forcible intervention by the developed states against the developing states but also to inhibit the former from taking forcible measures, if

D. Hansen, "The Political Economy of North-South Relations: How Much Change?" *International Organization* 29 (Autumn 1975): 921–47.

necessary, to defend themselves against the threat of desperate action by the latter. There is no apparent reason why we should accept this assumption. If we do not, the Western states need not be vulnerable to the threat of radically disruptive behavior. They may be vulnerable to certain measures developing states take that, though clearly measures of economic coercion, do not raise the prospect of force. But the effectiveness of such measures will largely depend, as already noted, on a degree of unity that itself remains uncertain.

When we consider the prospect of not only serious and widespread threats of economic coercion by the developing states but also the further prospect of threats of armed coercion, or terrorism, we move from the already unpersuasive to the implausible. It is perhaps the poverty of our imagination that prompts us to consider the prospect of nuclear terrorism that many have raised. The time may come when, as Robert Heilbroner writes, "the underdeveloped nations which have 'nothing' to lose will point their nuclear pistols at the heads of the passengers in the first-class coaches who have everything to lose." If that time should ever come, it might even be that some of the world's "first class passengers" would no longer resist the blandishments of the poor, not so much because the rich had become converted to the cause of the poor as because they no longer possessed the will to resist such blandishments. Given their recent behavior, it is perhaps not too strained to find in the present outlook of Western Europe and Japan at least the distant harbinger of a disposition that may one day give unexpected credibility to the threat of nuclear terrorism by the poor.

The much more likely prospect, however, is that well before the poor nations had developed a capability and will to threaten the rich nations with terrorist attacks, let alone with "wars of redistribution," the latter would have begun the process of a radical decoupling from the poor. The time this process would require and the extent to which it could be carried out must remain matters of controversy and uncertainty. But unless we are to assume that collectives will behave in the future as they have never behaved in the past, there is every reason for believing that the rich nations would make the effort to separate, and radically so, their destiny from that of the poor nations.

IV

These considerations may well be betrayed by events. Whether they are or not, it is necessary to take seriously the general thrust of the scenarios projected in preceding pages, for to the degree that these visions of the future gain acceptance, they become—by virtue of this acceptance—significant.

If we do take seriously the substance of the views portrayed above, what are the consequences for international order? Although the international system will remain one of self-help, the utility of what was once the most important form of self-help, and therefore the mainstay of such order as the international system traditionally possessed, will presumably continue to decline. At least, this would appear to be the prevailing view taken in the West today, particularly with respect to the relations between the developed and capitalist states and the developing countries.

At the same time, this decline in the utility of military power will not occur in the context of a system that is marked by declining conflicts of interest between developed and developing countries. Certainly, to the degree that the new egalitarianism becomes a force to be reckoned with, it does not foreshadow a diminution of competition over the goods states have regularly competed over in the past. On the contrary, in its demands for a new distribution of wealth and power—and, not least, of status—the challenge the new egalitarianism has raised holds out the prospect of conflict that is likely to be both intense and pervasive. If the principal bases of the traditional order are eroding, and are expected to erode even further, how will these conflicts be resolved? Indeed, does not the prospect beckon of an international system in which a growing number of conflicts may not be resolved at all?

Equality and Order

Thus we can see one of the principal consequences of the new egalitarianism and one of the central issues it must pose. If permitted, for whatever reasons, to run its promised course, the new egalitarianism promises to lead, as it is leading even today, to a growing disjunction between order and power; that is, to an international society in which the principal holders of power—at least among the developed and capitalist states—may no longer be the principal creators and guarantors of order. The potential bases of power will not somehow disappear or be radically transformed. At least, their disappearance or transformation is not foreseen by the new egalitarianism. As distinct from the view increasingly entertained by liberal elites in the West, the elites of the new states do not assume that the struggle for the "new" order will also be one characterized by the emergence of equally new, though more benign, forms of power. What they do appear to assume is that for a number of reasons the developed and capitalist states will be increasingly inhibited in their use of traditional forms of power, despite the fact that the structure of self-help will remain essentially unchanged.

It is in this sense that we may say that a practical consequence of the new egalitarianism is to lead to a growing disjunction between power and order, and that though the developed and capitalist states will remain for an indefinite period the principal holders of power, they will no longer be the principal creators and guarantors of order. The erosion of their position will reflect growing uncertainty—or skepticism—over the utility (effectiveness) and the legitimacy of the traditional forms of power—above all, military power. Given this uncertainty, a corresponding uncertainty will eventually arise over the nature of order itself which, should it persist, must lead to a further decline of the old order even while no new order has been firmly established. For the beneficiaries of the old order will no longer be willing to enforce the order of the past, while the challengers of the old order will remain—at least, for a transitional period—incapable of creating a new order. The disjunction between power and order will accordingly be characterized by a decline in both power and order. As long as the disjunction is not resolved, it threatens to lead to chaos; that is, to a situation where conflicting claims cannot be resolved because there is no consensus on the standards or norms for resolving these claims and where the power to impose a solution, in the absence of consensus, is either unavailable or simply not employed.

In this situation, it is not difficult to project a further consequence of the new egalitarianism. Since nature abhors a vacuum, the new equality also holds out the prospect of an international system in which the power position of the Soviet Union will be considerably enhanced, for the Russians are neither dependent in any significant way on the new states nor disposed to view their claims in the manner of Western elites. Nor have the spokesmen of the new egalitarianism been at pains to date to address their claims to the Soviet Union.* It is the dependent and vulnerable—and, of course, formerly colonial and presently neo-colonial—West that has been the principal object of their demands. The disjunction between power and order will accordingly be largely one-sided in its effects. Whether this prospective outcome is to be welcomed or decried is not at issue here. What is at issue is the problems it must raise to the degree it is realized.

There are many who will take exception even to this manner of formulating the consequences of the movement toward greater equality in international society, let alone to what they sense to be the implications of the formulation. Why speak of a growing disjunction between order and power, it will be asked, rather than of a changing order that is in turn both consequence and cause of a changing power? Moreover, why speak of the principal possessors of power that are no longer the principal creators and guarantors of order, if it is admitted that order implies power? True, convention sanctions the loose usage whereby one speaks of power that is no longer usable or effective. This manner of speaking is misleading, however, since power that is no longer usable or effective is no longer power in any meaningful sense.

* There are recent indications, however, that the exempted status heretofore accorded the Soviet Union may be changing.

Equality and Order

Thus, it is argued, no useful purpose is served by pointing to the markedly declining utility of traditional forms of power—above all, military power—as creating a separation between power and order. What is happening instead is that a new and more egalitarian order is emerging, in part because a form of power that was once decisive and pervasive is no longer so, or, at any rate, less so. In this view, then, to point to a growing disjunction between power and order betrays a retrogressive outlook and a yearning to return to the traditionally hierarchical system ordered primarily on the basis of relative military capability.

There is some merit to these considerations, if for no other reason than what may appear as order to one observer may appear as disorder to another. So it has always been, and we have no persuasive reason for believing that contemporary judgments are somehow free of this perennial bias. Unless the concept of order is reduced to the mere effectiveness with which power—whatever its ingredients and application—secures such behavior as its holders ordain, there is an unavoidable element of preference implicit in all judgments of what constitutes order. If this is true with respect to civil society, it is for obvious reasons all the more true with respect to international society. There is a very long tradition of looking upon international life as one of anarchy, and one that will remain anarchical in the absence of effective collective procedures. And even if the domestic analogy from which this view is drawn is rejected, the question remains as relevant today as ever, and perhaps even more relevant: how far may the domestic analogy be departed from without straining almost any reasonable concept of order to a breaking point?

It is not these qualifications, however, that form the principal objection to the position holding that there is a growing disjunction between power and order in state relations. After all, if there is an unavoidable element of subjectivity in all judgments of order, this is not to say that all such judgments are equally subjective. Nor is it to say that a disjunction between power and order cannot arise. We know from experience that such disjunctions may, and occasionally

95

do, arise. One arose, for example, during the 1930s when the principal holders of power (the United States included) were for a time no longer the effective guarantors of the order they had created after World War I. To be sure, this disjunction, like all others, could only be provisional in character. Either the old order will be reaffirmed by those who for the time continue to hold predominant power or a new order will be established by those seeking to displace the established power holders. But as long as the beneficiaries of the old dispensation remain unwilling to enforce the order they created and once guaranteed, and the challengers, though assaulting the old order, remain incapable of creating a new order, there seems no valid reason to deny the existence of a disjunction between power and order.

If this disjunction is nevertheless objected to in the present context, it is largely because of the assumption that power itself is changing and that, in consequence, the old order must change—and, in substantial measure, has already changed—with it. These changes are not considered provisional but permanent; they are not deemed reversible but irreversible. Thus, objection to the view holding to a growing disjunction between power and order centers on the alleged failure to recognize what Pierre Renouvin has termed the "underlying forces" at work in contemporary world politics. For it is these forces that are presumably constantly eroding the old order and the forms of power that maintained it. Today's increasingly interdependent world is found to result from weapons that can no longer protect, let alone aggrandize, the state; from a technology that no longer permits the "separate" state; from transnational economic and social actors that have come to function largely independently of the state; and from a process of industrial growth creating problems that cannot be resolved in isolation by the state. In almost all its variations, then, the theme of interdependence points to the state's growing loss of autonomy.

It will be clear that the interdependence we are concerned with here is not only economic but military-strategic as well. In the context of this discussion, the endless controversies among the experts over the meaning of interdependence need not detain us. The layman approaching the subject might instead usefully turn to any standard dictionary. "Interdependence," he will read, is a condition or state of "mutual dependence" or "dependence on each other." Thus interdependent relationships can normally be broken only at substantial cost to the parties involved. If this were not so, the parties would not be mutually dependent (though they still might be "related" in some measure and, accordingly, "affected" in some way by each other's actions). Of course, the costs of breaking interdependencies may—and usually will—vary considerably, just as they may—and usually will—be greater for one party than for another.*

What is of relevance in this context, however, is not so much the state's loss of autonomy as the egalitarian implications this loss conveys. Marked inequality—certainly radical inequality—is seen to threaten an interdependent society for the reason that interdependence is considered a synonym for vulnerability. A society made up of increasingly interdependent units is a society made up of increasingly vulnerable units. If the great moral imperative of the age is equality, as we are constantly told, an interdependent world that does

---

* All this occasions little difficulty. It is necessary to add, though, that there are two types of interdependence. In the one, defined above, interdependence is referred to as positive because the interests of the parties vary directly, though still perhaps quite unequally. Indeed, it is the inequality of the respective gains of each party from the relationship that may prove a cause of conflict. And it is for this reason that even a high degree of positive interdependence may nevertheless prove to be a cause of conflict. In the other kind of interdependence, referred to as negative, the interests of the parties vary inversely. What one party stands to gain, the other loses. An improvement in the position of one is assumed to result in a deterioration of the position of the other. Negative interdependence is, of course, a conflict or adversary relationship par excellence. Finally, there is a kind of interdependence between nuclear adversaries for which no term seems particularly appropriate. This is so because it may be assumed that, in attempting to resolve their conflict through force, what one side must lose the other side must also lose in equal degree. It is an interdependence not only of suffering but of equality in suffering. In the text the emphasis is on interdependence taken in the positive sense, though—to repeat—this interdependence may always prove a cause of conflict because of the unequal returns the respective parties draw from the relationship. The point is important since many seem to assume that positive interdependence, being a game of mixed interests rather than a zero-sum game, will tend to reduce the traditional conflicts of states. It may or may not do so. What matters is precisely the "mixture" of interests, or, at least, the perception of this mixture by the parties. If one party believes that the gains to the other are disproportionate, then conflict may follow even though the aggrieved party also benefits from interdependence. At present, demands for greater equality—whether domestic or international—are almost all made in a setting of positive interdependence.

not respond to this imperative is evidently a world with a very bleak future. Occasionally, proponents of interdependence are reluctant to acknowledge this point. Though almost without exception committed to the view that an increasing interdependence carries with it the promise of a decrease in coercion—certainly armed coercion—a distinction is drawn between the bearing of interdependence on equality and its bearing on peace. "It is important to remember," two leading students of the subject write, "that interdependence by no means implies equality. Interdependent relationships are more or less asymmetrical depending on the characteristics of issue-areas and the attitudes and interests of elites, as well as on the aggregate levels of power of the states involved." * But the point is not so much whether interdependent relationships are asymmetrical as it is whether or not blatant and continued asymmetries threaten interdependence, particularly in a system that, while remaining one of self-help, is characterized by growing demands for equality on the part of the victims of these asymmetries and growing reluctance to use power on the part of the beneficiaries of these asymmetries. When put in this way, the conclusion must be that in a world demanding greater equality, either present asymmetries marking interdependent relationships must be substantially reduced or interdependence must be jeopardized (with all that this is commonly alleged to imply).

It is of more than passing interest that the by now pervasive theme of interdependence is only seldom applied to the Soviet Union (or, for that matter, China), and with good reason. By this very omission we may conclude that interdependence is largely irrelevant to the state that will assuredly continue to play a major, and increasing, role in world politics. For the purpose of conventional political analysis, this qualification alone may well be regarded as critical. Still, one need not press this point. The qualifications to interdependence are considerable, even when kept to the rather abstract level its advocates appear to prefer. If in one sense modern weapons make all

* Robert O. Keohane and Joseph S. Nye, Jr., "International Interdependence and Integration" in Fred Greenstein and Nelson Polsby, eds., *Handbook of Political Science* (Reading, Mass.: Addison-Wesley, 1975), vol. 8, p. 367.

states vulnerable as never before, in another sense these weapons may confer a security on their possessors that states seldom enjoyed in the past. Indeed, for the great nuclear powers, nuclear-missile weapons have conferred what has heretofore proven unachievable— a surfeit of deterrent power. If in one sense technology—particularly communications—no longer permits the "separate state," in another sense technology gives the state making full use of it powers it previously rarely possessed. Moreover, the same technology that confers these powers also makes possible—at any rate, for the favored few—a policy akin to autarchy. Nor is it at all apparent that in a confrontation between the state and major transnational actor of the period, the multinational corporation, the state will find itself waging a losing battle. The multinational corporation has flourished, as Robert Gilpin notes, within the framework of a favorable political order.* Whether it will continue to flourish in the absence of political conditions that promoted its growth remains an open question. Finally, whether or not states pursue a policy of independence or interdependence, they must eventually face the problems attendant upon growth. But there is no compelling reason for believing these problems can only be resolved through the methods of interdependence, and, indeed, there are a number of reasons for believing quite the contrary. In sum, the forces commonly seen to be draining the state of its former autonomy are, for the most part, quite ambiguous in their significance.

V

Even if one accepts the view of an ever-rising interdependence occurring at the expense of the state, the prospect of a growing disjunction between power and order is not thereby excluded. It is excluded

---

* ". . . the success of the multinational corporation has been dependent upon a favorable political order. As this order changes, so will the fortunes of the multinationals" (Robert Gilpin, "Three Models of the Future," in Bergsten and Krause, eds., *World Politics and International Economics,* p. 49).

only if one assumes that interdependence itself is largely constitutive of order and that this order is self-maintaining, at least in the sense that its maintenance does not depend upon the threat or use of physical coercion. In fact, however, such interdependence as we have in international society today, although creating the need for a greater measure of order, provides no assurance that this need will be met, whether by a supposedly declining state or by some alternative institution(s). Indeed, if the state is being slowly but surely drained of its autonomy, as the believers in interdependence would have it, then, in the absence of effective alternative political institutions, what order international society has heretofore enjoyed must be jeopardized. Surely the order of the past generation must be jeopardized, since the state that has presided over it is presumably no longer capable of doing so.

If the interdependence advocates do not see matters in this light, it is because they assume that interdependence itself is largely constitutive of order, that an interdependent world must establish its own set of rules and constraints, and that this order does not include force, the *ultima ratio* that characterized and defined the traditional system. Obviously, the new system will still be one largely dominated by self-help. What else could it be in the absence of supranational institutions? But the self-help of interdependence will show a far more benign face than the self-help of the traditional system, and it will do so because the threat or use of force is destructive of interdependence. Is this apparent circularity of the argument a fundamental flaw? No, provided a sufficiently high value is attached by *all* participants to those consequences held to follow from interdependence.*

* All of this has, of course, a familiar ring. The view that interdependence is itself constitutive of order and that the power needed to uphold this order is both minimal and benign appears as the most recent version of what may be termed Cobdenite liberalism as applied to international affairs. It should not be confused with the liberalism of the classical economists; that is, with the writings of David Hume and Adam Smith and their followers through John Stuart Mill. Of the classical economists, Lionel Robbins has written that ''there is little evidence that they often went beyond the test of national advantage as a criterion of policy, still less that they were prepared to contemplate the dissolution of national bonds. If you examine the ground on which they recommended free trade, you will find that it is always in terms of a more produc-

Equality and Order

To be sure, the more cautious prophets of the new order of inter-dependence readily concede that the emergence of this order is both complicated and threatened by the persistence of "obsolete" forms of power (and, of course, by the persistence of equally obsolete attitudes that have yet to adjust to the requirements of an interdependent world). One of them writes: "Indeed, if countries with nuclear weapons and other powerful military capabilities invoked their military superiority for purposes of facing down opponents in any type of conflict situation, then military force and militarized diplomacy—although bad currency—in a kind of Gresham's law of international politics, would tend to drive out the good currency of cooperative and limited coalition-building." * But this admitted tension between the old and the new is seen as unavoidable in a period of transition. It can, and in all likelihood will, be overcome as the forces of inter-dependence continue to erode the already weakened position of the state.

Although it is clear that we are dealing here not only with an analysis but with a prescription, it is the "to be" rather than the "ought to be" that primarily concerns us. What is the basis for believing that this tension between the old and the new will be resolved in favor of the new? It will not do to respond by pointing once again to "underlying forces" the significance of which are, as noted, quite ambiguous. At best, these forces leave one on uncertain ground and, if

---

tive use of *national* resources. . . . It was the consumption of the national economy that they regarded as the end of economic activity" (*The Theory of Economic Policy in English Classical Political Economy* [London: Macmillan, 1952], pp. 10–11). There is no suggestion in the classical economists that free trade is somehow constitutive of order and, in consequence, places limits on the autonomy of the state. On the contrary, it is the state, the political framework, that is seen to make possible a liberal trading system and to guarantee the order and security without which such a system could not function. In Cobdenite liberalism these assumptions are very nearly abandoned, if not reversed. Free trade is largely constitutive of order, an order that responds to individual (consumption) interests. The state that is so far from being the creator of whatever harmony or consensus exists in international society is the prime agent of conflict and disorder. The great necessity, then, is to place increasing limits on the state's autonomy so as to permit the harmonious interests of individuals and, in the modern setting, of apolitical transnational associations to find full expression.

* Seyom Brown, "The Changing Essence of Power," *Foreign Affairs* 51 (January 1973): 294.

anything, suggest that the tension, rather than being resolved in favor of the new, may only become more pronounced. If this is so, it serves to strengthen the view of a growing disjunction between power and order with all that this disjunction must portend. Even in the new order of interdependence, it seems only reasonable to assume that conflicts of interest will arise and that, as the oil crisis has demonstrated, a growing interdependence will itself be productive of many very serious conflicts of interest. How will such conflicts be resolved if the traditional means for resolving them are to be neither employed nor meaningfully threatened? To respond that the means of conflict resolution will increasingly approximate the means of resolving conflicts within the state assumes a degree of consensus international society has not known in the past and clearly does not know at present. But this in turn assumes a formative agent of consensus—and, indeed, of conscience—that heretofore at least has invariably been the state (and not, as a still regnant liberal outlook insists, an elusive "society").

VI

If we are plainly not already in a consensual world, is there plausible reason to believe that we are moving toward one? Interdependence cannot of itself provide such reason, since it is as much a source of conflict as of consensus, if not more. It is a source of conflict not only because it promotes insecurity and competition while failing to provide the means for assuaging insecurity and setting bounds to competition. Even if interdependence is seen to result in benefits to all parties, these benefits may nevertheless vary considerably and particularly in a world made up of states at very different levels of economic development. In the absence of agreement on the distribution of benefits derived from interdependence, a sensitivity to what are perceived as substantial disparities in benefits will provide at least as great a source of conflict as of consensus. The most insistent demands for greater equality have all too frequently arisen precisely in situations where, though all parties are benefiting from interdependency, some parties are perceived as benefiting disproportionately to others. If these perceptions, and the resulting demands for greater equity, are a commonplace within relatively stable and cohesive domestic societies, as they are today, it is scarcely surprising that even more insistent demands should arise in an interdependent international society that enjoys almost none of the bonds of domestic society.

Can development provide what interdependence cannot provide? Many apparently think so and find in the very universality of commitment to the cause of development the consensus that may serve as the foundation of a new order. In our time development expresses a basic imperative of human solidarity, Jean-Marie Domenach declares; "it binds states together in an agreement which can no longer be simply a pact of non-aggression, but must be one of mutual assistance. . . ." * But the issues that interdependence raises are also in large measure the issues development must raise, however widespread the approval development elicits in principle. This is so if only for the reason that the commitment to development, if taken at all seriously, is evidently a commitment to a greater measure of equality. Although development may and does mean many things, one thing it surely means to its legions of supporters is a world in which material disparities will be less marked than they are at present. No doubt, those who go so far as to equate development with equality exaggerate. The exaggeration is a pardonable one, however, in view of the importance equality occupies in the development imperative.

Unless we assume that the greater measure of global equality expected to attend development will result almost entirely from the indigenous efforts of the developing countries themselves, the development of the latter evidently entails a steady transfer of wealth—at

---

* Jean-Marie Domenach, "Our Moral Involvement in Development," in *United Nations: The Case for Development* (New York: Praeger, 1973), p. 131.

any rate, of future wealth—from the rich to the poor countries.* Is it reasonable to expect such transfer to occur voluntarily as a consequence of some transcendent consensus on the desirability of development? It would not seem so. Certainly, it would not seem so if we take as our point of reference the only experience we have. Within major Western democratic states, the efforts that have been made to achieve a greater measure of socio-economic equality have met with considerable resistance. Yet these efforts have been undertaken within nation-states that have a long history and enjoy some measure of cohesiveness and solidarity.

The paradox and the difficulty attending all movements toward achieving greater equality are that in large measure they must presuppose the very conditions they seek to achieve. The great end ultimately sought through equality is fraternity; in Tawney's expression, the society of fellowship. Yet the achievement of this end remains unattainable without the preexistent measure of cohesiveness and solidarity that safeguards against the conflicts raised by the demands for greater equality, conflicts that may well prove destructive of fellowship. No major Western state has yet managed to resolve this paradox satisfactorily for the reason that none has enjoyed the moral resources, the degree of consensus and sympathy, requisite for its resolution. Instead, the quest for equality has been met by the promise of equal opportunity, by the expectation that everyone's material condition may be constantly improved through growth, and by the recognition that everyone must be insured at least a minimal level of subsistence. Whether one regards this record as commendable or deplorable, as a substantial realization of equality or a betrayal of it, is not at issue here. Of relevance is the point that this, in rough approximation, is the historic response Western democratic states have made to demands for greater equality. In part, this response—the provision of a minimal standard of subsistence—was made only after a relatively high level of development had been

* Some will object to the use of the term "transfer" here. There is no need to argue the point. What is clear is that greater equality of opportunity, and of condition, is to be brought about by, at the very least, a new distribution of future global wealth. Whether this relinquishment by the rich of their present share of growth may be viewed as a transfer of wealth to the poor need not be insisted upon.

achieved. Even so, its recognition has come slowly and, to many, quite inadequately.

If this experience has any relevance for the problem of global inequality, we can only expect that the development imperative, whatever the degree of consensus it elicits in principle, will in reality provide an acute and continuing source of conflict. Given the notorious lack of cohesiveness and solidarity of international society, the demand to reduce present disparities of income and wealth would produce conflict even in quite favorable circumstances. For even in quite favorable circumstances, international economic relationships would still be relationships of equity with their clearly redistributive overtones. Moreover, the prime movers in the demand for equality will be states. It is through the existing framework of states, sovereign and independent, that disparities in income and wealth are to be reduced, if they are to be reduced at all. Is there reason to expect that the claims of underdeveloped states to greater equality will be moderated with a steady improvement in their standards of living? Here again, if the experience of domestic society is at all relevant, the answer cannot prove comforting in its implications for international conflict.

It is a well-known theme of conservatives that the issue of equality grows more acrimonious and demands for greater equality grow more insistent as the poor begin to improve their socio-economic status and to see the possibilities heretofore hidden from them. But the theme also happens to be borne out by experience, and candid egalitarians have always acknowledged, even while defending it, the growth of resentment against inequality that attends the growth of equality. It is one of the great egalitarians of the century who wrote that the determination to end disabilities deemed needless and advantages deemed preferential "has its source, not in material misery, but in sentiments which the conquest of the grosser forms of poverty has given room to grow." * Recently, a champion of greater global equality has warned in unequivocal terms against the belief that a

* R. H. Tawney, *Equality* (4th ed.; London: Allen and Unwin Ltd., 1952), p. 225. Of course, what constitutes "needless disabilities" and "preferential advantages" varies with the growth of equality itself.

modest rise in living standards among the underdeveloped nations will moderate their claims and thereby promote a world with less conflict.* Nor is the reason for the sharpened intolerance of inequality that attends the growth of equality to be found simply in the sentiments that rising expectations bring, sentiments that readily make remaining inequalities appear intolerable. In part, this rising determination to end inequality is to be explained by the conviction that the position of the privileged is no longer secure once concessions have been wrested from them by whatever means. The significance of this conviction will of course vary according to circumstances. In international society it is bound to prove quite significant, given the circumstances normally marking the concession of interests by states— let alone the concession of vital interests. It was entirely to be expected that the major OPEC states should view the manner in which concessions were wrung from the developed and capitalist states as indicative of a no longer secure power position. And it is to be expected that if the latter states continue to behave as they have behaved to date, the former, acting according to this view, will press for a still greater measure of ''equality.''

Nor will this greater measure of equality find expression only in the reduction of present disparities in income and wealth. Once again, we need to remind ourselves that, from the vantage point of the new states, the inequalities development is expected to correct are also inequalities of power and status. Indeed, they are probably *above all* inequalities of power and status. As such, the redress of inequalities in income and wealth is not only ranked lower in significance than is the redress of inequalities in power and status; the prime purpose perhaps of redressing the former inequalities is to redress the latter. The elites of the new states have not sought to obscure the essential meaning that equality has for them. Instead, it is Western elites that have insistently sought to do so. In this respect, it is symptomatic that the assumed consensus on development is commonly seen in the West as a consensus on individual consumption

* Myrdal, "The World Poverty Problem," p. 34.

standards, or welfare, largely divorced from the power and status of collectives. By taking this view, while minimizing the difficulties raised above, its adherents are able to maintain their otherwise mystifying optimism over the consequences of development and to persist in the belief that development will prove, on balance, a source of consensus rather than of conflict. Whereas the ends of consumption and welfare may be seen as inherently cooperative and unifying, the ends of power and status must be seen as competitive and divisive. For consumption and welfare are not inherently exclusive goods, particularly in a world that holds out the prospect of relatively open-ended growth, whereas power and status are very close to being so.* The consensus on development, if it is to be taken as a serious prospect, must also comprise a consensus on power and status. In a new distribution of wealth there will also be a new distribution of power and status. But if the former may possibly occur without the rich and powerful paying a substantial price, the latter, and consequent, distribution is bound to occur at the heavy expense of the now rich. In this respect, and it is all-important, the new egalitarianism clearly portends a competitive rather than cooperative future, and the same must be said of development generally.

These considerations suggest that the development process—as interdependence—holds out the promise of far more conflict than consensus, even accepting the assumption of relatively open-ended growth. It is this assumption that provided the foundation for Western-inspired postwar development programs, just as it is this assumption that accounted for the optimism placed in these programs. Given a moderate amount of competence and will on the part of governments of developing countries, a convergence of per-capita growth rates was expected to result in the not-too-distant future from

* What Hobbes said of glory—we use the term "status" or "prestige"—may also be said of power. ". . . Glory is like honor, if all men have it, no man hath it, for they consist in comparison and precellence" (Sir William Molesworth, ed., *The English Works of Thomas Hobbes* [Aalen, Germany: Scientia, 1962], vol. 2, *De Cive,* ch. 1, sec. 2, p. 5). The games of power and status are essentially competitive games. This is why the proponents of interdependence and of consensus give them short shrift in their visions of the future.

modest aid infusions and technology transfers. Convergent per-capita growth rates, in turn, would eventually lead to per-capita income levels that, if not equalized globally, would still exceed the levels of income prevailing at the time in the developed states.

This view persists in some quarters even today, but it is clearly a declining faith. Population growth alone has dealt it a very severe blow. The goal of converging per-capita growth rates has been moved from the not-too-distant to the indefinite future, and levels of per-capita income once entertained have simply been abandoned. In the meantime, disillusionment within Western countries over the results of development efforts in many Southern states has been met by rising resentment of the poor over what is seen as a commitment by the rich that is at once no more than of token significance and yet increasingly unbearable for the interventionist pressures it is often felt to bring.

In retrospect, it is apparent that the favored solution for international inequality was a variation of the favored solution for domestic inequality. Even if the rather elusive, though ubiquitous, "gap" was not substantially closed, it would not matter terribly, it was believed, if the standard of living of all rose dramatically. This proposition is far from self-evident, again as domestic experience has shown. What Charles Frankel has observed in the domestic context ("a man does not have to be poor to be disadvantaged; he merely needs to be poorer than somebody else") may prove no less relevant in the international context.

At any rate, the favored solution of an open-ended growth process has been called into question, and, in consequence, the faith that found in development the promise of a new order has been shaken. For the appearance of constraints on growth changes the entire setting in which development and the reduction of global inequalities were to have taken place. What once appeared as not only a plausible but a painless goal no longer does so. Nor is it enough to respond that present constraints on growth will not prove to be lasting, that what we are confronted with is a short-to-medium term problem likely to be resolved, depending upon the particular constraint, over the next ten to thirty years. The long term may produce catastrophe. On the other hand, the long term may find solutions to problems that appear next to insoluble today. We cannot know. But it is not the long term that concerns us. It is the near term, for that is the only term statecraft responds to, if indeed it responds to that.

VII

Given the circumstances likely to prevail in the near term, the need for order will prove not less but greater than in the past. It will prove greater because interdependence creates relationships and development gives rise to claims that, if not somehow resolved, may easily lead to chaos. The oil crisis, beginning with the Arab embargo and the reaction of the developed states to the embargo, strikingly illustrates this need without affording any assurance it will be met in the future. If it is not, the reason will be that the strong are no longer willing to enforce the order of the past, while the weak who have challenged this order are incapable of creating a new order. Even so, the failure to enforce the order of the past will still mean, on balance, the relinquishment of interest by the strong.

Is it plausible to expect this anomalous situation to persist? If not quite plausible, it is still possible, if only for the reason that this situation will remain critically dependent upon political and moral perceptions that may yet transform today's possibility into tomorrow's reality. To be sure, these perceptions are not of equal moment. Nor are they directly relevant to each and every conflict of interest between the developed and capitalist states of the North and the states of the South. Moreover, they are identified much more with elite groups in the North than with the publics at large. Still, their general significance today for the response the new egalitarianism has evoked cannot be in serious doubt. Implicit throughout the preceding discussion, they are: a rising disinclination to use or to threaten force, whether from the belief that force is no longer expedient or from the conviction that force is no longer a legitimate instrument or, more likely, from a combination of the two; a view that the developed states are in many respects highly vulnerable; a persuasion that growing interdependence is threatened by inequalities that, if allowed to persist, will result in generalized chaos or war; a commitment generally to reducing international inequalities, though without a clear idea of—or, for that matter, interest in—the effects a redistribution of wealth would have on the redistribution of world power; and, finally, a sense of guilt over a past for which we are now thought to be paying the inevitable price.

It is against this outlook that the response to OPEC actions may largely be understood.* The oil crisis is the clearest indication we have to date of the way the new egalitarianism may be expected to work if given free rein. It is not easy, however, to see it being given free rein in the future. A political-moral outlook that once proved not only relatively costless but congenial to Western interests is bound to be challenged once it is apparent that if acted upon the result will mean a world over which we will have decreasing control at increasing cost. For if a large portion of Western liberal elites find no more difficulty in distinguishing between the United States and Bangladesh than between California and Mississippi, it is safe to say that the general public continues to find a great deal of difficulty and that democratic governments will continue to prove responsive to the distinction the public draws between its collective welfare and the welfare of those outside the state.

There are even reasons for believing that this distinction may be drawn more sharply in the future than in the recent past. One reason, paradoxically enough, is the growing demand for greater equality

* This response could scarcely condemn the ends (development, equality, etc.) professedly sought by the oil producing states. Moreover, condemnation of the means employed to reach these ends must prove less than persuasive if made largely on the ground that the present oil price is the administered price of a cartel. Quite apart from the consideration that pre-OPEC oil prices were also the administered prices of a cartel, the prices of a large number of industrial goods developing states must import are, in effect, administered prices. It is very late in the day for Western liberals to object to price-fixing simply because it is undertaken by states.

within many of the developed states. That in America this demand may be expected to mount in intensity is forecast by champions and critics of equality alike.* Yet a more egalitarian America need not mean a greater willingness to reduce global inequalities of wealth, all the more so to the extent that egalitarianism takes place within the cultural and value setting of "traditional" America.† In these circumstances, a case may be made for an America that shows no more, and perhaps even less, disposition to concern itself with poverty abroad than the America of today. We may expect that those experiencing improved material well-being will, despite their improvement, insist upon defining "needs" in terms of "wants." This being so, the demands for further improvement are, if anything, likely to increase. These considerations, moreover, are only underlined by the possibility that industrial growth within the developed countries may decline in the years ahead, however modestly. For even a modest slowdown in industrial growth will intensify the problem of equality for domestic societies whose social stability is so centrally dependent upon economic expansion.

If the new egalitarianism is to overcome the expected resistance of publics in the developed states, it must do so in part at least by an appeal to justice that will eventually strike a responsive chord in those who are asked to recognize and act upon a conception of the common good that transcends the bounds of the state. Does the new egalitarianism, despite its apparent insistence that the rich will only act through self-interest, hold out such appeal? And if it does not, or does so insufficiently, is there an emergent ethic entertained by elites

---

* For the former, see Herbert J. Gans, *More Equality* (New York: Pantheon, 1973). For the latter, Daniel Bell, *The Coming of Post-Industrial Society* (New York: Basic Books, 1973). Gans writes (p. xii) that "more equality must come because Americans favor it and because America cannot function in the long run without more equality." Bell (p. 425) finds the redefinition of equality—from equality of opportunity to equality of result—"the central value problem of post-industrial society."

† As Herbert J. Gans (*More Equality*, pp. xvi, 25) is so persuaded. He writes that egalitarianism in the future America "will not be based on altruism," that "it will be individualistic," and that "it does not presuppose that people are ready to stop competing for material or nonmaterial gain."

111

in the West that may prove sufficiently persuasive in breaking down the distinction publics continue to draw between their collective welfare and the welfare of those outside the state? May the order of the past and, for that matter, of the present be transformed without excessive conflict and the serious threat of chaos by a moral transformation that will obviate the need to submit the claims of the new egalitarianism simply to the arbitrament of power?

IV

Equality and Justice

I

W E HAVE ARGUED that if the new egalitarianism is permitted to run its promised course it can be expected to lead to a growing disjunction between order and power; that is, to an international society in which the principal holders of power—at least among the developed and capitalist states—will no longer be the principal creators and guarantors of order. Whether this prospective outcome of the new equality is to be welcomed or decried is not at issue. What is at issue is that the disjunction between order and power must be seen against the background of an international system in which the need for order has not declined but, if anything, has increased. The need for order has increased because interdependence and development create relationships and give rise to claims that, if not somehow resolved, may easily lead to chaos. Yet it is not easy to see how conflicting claims will be resolved if the means traditionally employed for resolving them are to undergo progressive erosion while little is put in their place. Certainly, interdependence can scarcely be considered a satisfactory substitute for the traditional instruments of order. In itself, interdependence is not constitutive of order. It is not even a condition of order, save in the special sense that it magnifies the need for order. At the same time, it provides no assurance that the need will be met.

The new egalitarianism not only promises a growing disjunction between power and order; it also reflects a disjunction between order and justice. In some measure, it is the latter disjunction that must be seen to explain the former. If the prospect beckons of a world in which the principal holders of power are no longer the principal creators and guarantors of order, one critical reason is a widespread conviction that the present international order is in many respects unjust. There is of course nothing novel or surprising in the fact that an order is seen as unjust by those who feel that they have been denied their rightful share of its benefits. What is novel and surprising is the apparent perception of injustice by many who have enjoyed and continue to enjoy a favored position in this order. For it is not only the elites of the developing states who insistently question the justice of the present international order; it is increasingly the elites of the developed and capitalist states as well. Both the new egalitarianism of the South and the new political sensibility of the West converge in their condemnation of present international inequalities of income and wealth—and, consequently, of power.

It is this extraordinary convergence on the issue of the justice—or rather the injustice—of the present international system that must in substantial measure account for the growing disjunction between order and power, a disjunction that has been given striking illustration by the oil crisis. No doubt, the disinclination today among the developed and capitalist states to threaten or use force even when vital interests are jeopardized has other important roots, not the least of which is the belief that force is no longer an expedient means save in the most extreme circumstances. This belief has in turn exercised no little influence on the illegitimacy with which force is increasingly viewed today, particularly when employed by a great power against a small and weak state. Moreover, once the logic of collective equality was generally accepted and acted upon, the inevitable effect was to condemn intervention by a great power in the affairs of small states, often quite irrespective of the nature of the interests involved.

Even so, these reasons cannot adequately account for a marked decline in the propensity of the strong to threaten or to employ force against the weak—and, of equal significance, a decline in the propensity of the strong to take severe economic sanctions against the weak. In a society that remains as rudimentary and lacking in both cohesiveness and consensus as international society, a growing unwillingness to defend important interests—if necessary, by the threat or use of force—is surely in some measure an indication that the legitimacy of these interests has itself been called into question. In the case of the response to OPEC actions by Western elites, this last consideration was apparent from the start. A refusal to contemplate force reflected, among other things, the conviction that the interests to be preserved through force were themselves suspect insofar as they formed part of a larger order that has served to sustain radical disparities in income and wealth.

If the new political sensibility of Western liberal elites proves to be more than a transient mood, we may well be at the beginning of a significant shift in wealth and power as between the major developed states of the West and those who until recently formed the mere objects of history. But this shift, should it occur, is still not to be identified with the qualitative change that Western liberal elites increasingly project. As earlier observed, a shift in power, however far-reaching, is not to be confused with a change in the "essence" of power; a new international hierarchy is not to be mistaken for the disappearance of hierarchy; and a global redistribution of income and wealth is not to be equated with a "new beginning" in history if this redistribution is largely effected by, and in the name of, states. It is not the essential structure of the international system that the new egalitarianism has challenged, but the distribution of wealth and power within this system. Viewed from one perspective, this challenge may seem revolutionary, as indeed it is. Viewed from another and yet more profound perspective, this challenge appears altogether traditional. This is true not only of the strategies pursued by those who demand a greater share of wealth and power but also of the moral claims that serve to buttress this demand.

I I

The moral basis of the claims the new egalitarianism has addressed to the developed countries reflects the way in which present inequalities are seen to have arisen. If the division of the world into the developed and the underdeveloped is largely the result of a system that for so long deprived the underdeveloped of their independence, obstructed their path toward development, and denied them the true value of their rightful inheritance (natural resources), then one moral basis for claims to resource transfers today—whatever the forms these transfers may take—is apparent. Though given a variety of expression, the principle of justice invoked in support of these claims is one of reparations for past wrongs. In many respects, moreover, an exploitative "past" is found to have persisted into the present. Thus the OPEC states have sought in part to justify their recent actions by pointing to the history of the past twenty-five years, a history that is interpreted in such a way as to entitle them today to what is in effect a form of reparations. This is, for example, the well-known view of the Shah of Iran, who finds the present prosperity of Europe and Japan to be based on a generation of cheap fuel.* In the 1974 United Nations Declaration on the Establishment of a New Economic Order, the theme of reparations, though never directly alluded to, forms the pervasive justification for a new equality that appears to entail as many duties for the developed states as it does rights for the underdeveloped states.

On occasion, it is true, the demand for greater equality is placed on a very different moral basis. The obligation of the rich countries to assist the underdeveloped, and particularly the very poor, states has been expressed in terms of a larger and common good that finds

* This claim has found a responsive echo in the West. Geoffrey Barraclough writes that "the virtually continuous economic growth among the industrial nations of the West since the early 1950's was subsidized, and probably made possible, by the oil-producing countries" ("The Great World Depression I," *New York Review of Books* [January 23, 1975], p. 22). Barraclough cites approvingly the Shah's remarks as well as the much quoted comment of Giscard d'Estaing that in the oil crisis we are witnessing "the revenge on Europe for the 19th century" (and, apparently, the mid-twentieth century as well). In a subsequent essay, "Wealth and Power: The Politics of Oil and Food" (Ibid., August 7, 1975, p. 30), Barraclough ostensibly dismisses the reparations argument by declaring that: "It is not so much wrong as irrelevant. The West has as much right—no more and no less—to defend the existing system as the Third World has to attack it and pull it down. The question is, of course, at what cost." In fact, however, the entire thrust of Barraclough's article belies this stance of grand detachment, since his identification with the Third World and its claims is apparent throughout.

its ultimate expression in the sense of a shared humanity. In a recent statement to this effect, Indira Gandhi has urged the affluent nations to entertain the perspective not of charity but "of promoting positive cooperation for the larger good . . . the uplifting of three-quarters of the world which lives in want." * Yet expressions to this effect on the part of the elites of the new states are rather infrequent. Nor is this surprising. However attractive may be the appeal to Western elites of a solidarity that transcends the confines of the state, that appeal can have little attractiveness to elites of most of the new states. For the latter, it is not the vision of a sudden (and qualitative) extension of sympathy culminating in a shared humanity that will facilitate the ordeal of rapid development; it is the vision of a far more limited solidarity that is at once given tangible expression by and enforcement through the state.

The vision of a shared humanity is one thing for those who have long enjoyed the sense of status and worth that is largely conferred, for better or worse, by the independent state. It is quite another thing for those who have only recently achieved collective independence and whose sense of status and hunger for recognition as equals are still far from appeased. Similarly, it is one thing for those who have long played a salient role in history, largely by virtue of having achieved that independence and solidarity for which the state has been indispensable, to invoke today the imperative of human solidarity. It is quite another thing for peoples who have been the objects of history rather than its subjects to respond to this imperative. Before those who have only recently, and then with uncertainty, entered history can proceed to the stage of mankind, they must first pass through the stage of the state.

The appeal to a shared humanity (or to human solidarity, the brotherhood of man, etc.) not only places primary emphasis on the individual, and on individual equality, an emphasis that, as already observed, can have but limited attraction to the new states; it also suggests that the response to demands for greater economic equality

* *New York Times,* December 31, 1974.

is, after all, in the nature of a concession on the part of the developed states. This concession may be couched in terms of duty, but whatever the precise moral formulation, there will remain the psychological reality of a concession that can only confirm for the recipient a sense of inequality. It may be argued that resource transfers, though taking the form of reparations, must also be seen by the new and underdeveloped states as a concession. Even so, such transfers are a concession that more readily preserves the sense—or the illusion—of equality, in that reparations are not something merely given but something given back that was unjustly taken in the first place. The claim to resource transfers as a form of reparations suggests an equality that might have been had it not been for the depredations by the now rich. It represents the hardest possible "moral bargain" that the poor can strike.

It is for these reasons that the reparations claim, however it is expressed, may be expected to find continued favor in the moral armament of the new egalitarianism. That claim, we are often reminded, is not without its perils for the claimant. Not only does it fuel a politics of resentment for the claimant, but it must ultimately provoke a negative reaction even on the part of those accused who are initially disposed to entertain the claim of reparations. Thus one writer, though otherwise sympathetic to the new egalitarianism, warns: "The conscience cannot go on feeling remorse for very long; it seeks to eliminate the sensation by turning against those who remind it of its guilt; when it thinks it has undergone sufficient penitence, it becomes irritated at not finding its former adversary in a similar virtuous mood. Soon, the accused turns into an accuser and criticizes the underdeveloped country and former colony for not being able to make proper use of its independence." *

If this admonition cannot simply be dismissed, it is scarcely compelling. It is quite true that the psychology of reparations sustains a politics of resentment that must risk antagonizing those against whom it is directed. But where development must take place the hard

* Jean-Marie Domenach, "Our Moral Involvement in Development," in *United Nations: The Case for Development* (New York: Praeger, 1973), p. 127.

way, rather than being presented on an oil platter, a politics of resentment will in some measure at least prove difficult to avoid. The easiest objects of such resentment will predictably be in most instances the industrial and capitalist states of the West. In the cases of governments that fail to make significant progress in raising standards of living, yet are under increasing pressure to do so if only because of burgeoning populations, the reparations theme may prove particularly useful. How better to explain their failure than by pointing to an international system that for so long retarded their development and, for that matter, continues to do so?

III

These considerations must of course be set apart from the intrinsic validity of claims to reparations. What are the circumstances that validate claims to reparations, however expedient it may be to press such claims? In principle, there is little difficulty in answering this question. The claim to reparations is justified in response to wrongful and injurious action. But what is the nature of the wrongful and injurious action that validates claims to reparations? The standard response, as we know, is action that constitutes exploitation. Here again, however, one question only serves to provoke another. What is essential to comprise a relationship of exploitation? Clearly, it will not do to respond by saying that exploitation is inherent in any relationship between unequals, for there are any number of relationships between unequals that we do not normally consider relationships of exploitation. Inequality may and does provide the necessary condition for exploitation, but it cannot be identified with exploitation, even where those who are unequal are so by virtue of being at very different levels of development.

In a recent discussion of this protean term, Barrington Moore, although recognizing the "penumbra of emotive vagueness" marking its use, nevertheless concludes it is possible to give exploitation "a meaning independent of the feelings, preferences, and even whims of the parties to any given social relationship." "As a useful working definition," he writes, "we can say that exploitation forms part of an exchange of goods and services when (1) the goods and services exchanged are quite obviously not of equivalent value, and (2) one party to the exchange uses a substantial degree of coercion." In this view, it is not the inequality of the parties as such that determines exploitation but the manner in which inequality is expressed. Moore freely acknowledges the difficulties that in practice attend the determination of "equivalence," but he assumes that "a relatively disinterested observer . . . could make adequate distinctions most of the time. To believe otherwise forces one to hold that human society has never been and never *can* be based on anything but a mixture of force and fraud." *

It seems to me that Moore's assumption and conclusion are open to question. On the notorious difficulties of establishing equivalence, little need be said here save to remind ourselves that—notwithstanding the claims of liberals and Marxists alike—the notion of equivalence is socially determined, hence normative in character. This notion is not objective in the sense that it is somehow inherent or immanent in the nature of social—or economic—relationships. No doubt a "relatively disinterested observer" could determine equivalence—or the absence thereof—once given the socially relevant standards. Experience does not vindicate the view that such determination can be made in the absence of agreed-upon criteria. And it is precisely the absence of agreed-upon criteria for determining equivalence that is normally at issue. Certainly, it is at issue in the claims of underdeveloped states for reparations.

Even if the determination of equivalence should prove next to impossible, it does not follow that all social relationships must be based on a mixture of force and fraud. Indeed, there is no reason why exploitation cannot be defined as a relationship in which, to quote Moore again, "one party to the exchange uses a substantial degree of

* Barrington Moore, *Reflections on the Causes of Human Misery* (Boston: Beacon Press, 1972), pp. 53, 54.

coercion." To be sure, the concept of coercion is not without its own difficulties. But coercion has, despite these difficulties, an objectivity that equivalence does not have, and this is surely the case if we concentrate on the most important manifestations of coercion—the threat or use of force. So, too, fraud has an objectivity that equivalence does not and cannot have. A fraudulent relationship, it is agreed, is one based on the element of deception. What is common to both force and fraud is that they constitute relationships that presumably would not be entered into freely (in almost any sense of the term) by one party to the relationship. Equally, in both cases one party is deprived of some value against his will. In the case of force, however, this need not be a wrongful deprivation if the value taken by force was wrongfully obtained in the first place.

Are we then to accept claims of reparations where such claims are based on relationships in which one party has evidently been made the object of substantial coercion, particularly in the form of the threat or use of force? Of course, we *may* do so in the case of most of the underdeveloped states. If we do, however, we must at the very least be clear that these are claims based on moral, not legal, grounds. Prior to the contemporary period there was little, if anything, that forbade a Western state from threatening or using force against a people not considered as constituting a recognized subject of international law. And even if so recognized by international law, the latter still permitted ample scope for the threat or use of force.

As a moral basis for claims of reparations, it is equally the case that coercion—even in its extreme forms—cannot provide such basis unless we are to read present moral standards back into the past. What was true for the international law of an earlier period was also true for international morality. In the period that extended, for all practical purposes, from the origins of the state system down to the interwar years, a relationship based on a "substantial measure of coercion" was not considered for that reason as illegitimate by international society. The prevailing notions of legitimacy—naturally enough, the product of Western powers—did not condemn coercion exercised over the "backward" peoples of the world. On the contrary, until at least World War I the use of coercive methods against such peoples was considered justified, and certainly if the purpose was to improve the conditions of those against whom coercion might be employed. To those who determined what constituted legitimate behavior, what mattered was not the employment of coercion—including force—but the purpose and results of coercion. We shall return to this point presently.

There is a still larger, if not always an apparent, issue that is inevitably raised when claims for reparations are based on the contention that such disparities in income and wealth as exist today grew out of relationships based largely on force. We are dealing with a system of relations that historically has not only been centrally based on force but that has *institutionalized* force as a method for effecting change. If the position is to be taken today that such change as was effected by force cannot be regarded as legitimate, and must give rise to valid claims for reparations, then these claims may well go very far toward unraveling the entire system. It is not only the material aspects of the status quo but the territorial as well that fall within this challenge. In this respect, the difficulty of the reparations claim is not simply that it is a backward-looking one (how far back?) but that if it is based on force, *simpliciter,* it must open up a Pandora's box.*

How the new states will eventually come to view this Pandora's box will depend upon interest. Of this, we have already had several examples in the form of territorial disputes. Thus, in the forcible Indian seizure of Goa in 1961, the Indian government justified its action by pointing out that Portuguese possession of Goa was simply a case of "standing aggression," though lasting for four centuries, and a question of "getting rid of the last vestiges of colonialism." But this was not the Indian government's position in the territorial dispute with China; the Indian border territories China claimed had admittedly been the result of coercion applied at the turn of the century

* It is for this reason, among others, that Julius Stone asks: "After how many generations, and on what terms, could collective moral indebtedness in justice be written off, and the past left to bury its dead?" (Stone, "Approaches to the Notion of International Justice" in *The Future of the International Legal Order, vol. 1: Trends and Patterns,* Richard A. Falk and Cyril E. Black, eds. [1969], p. 70.)

by the British against a weak Chinese government. In the latter case, the results of colonialism were considered to have created the basis for legitimate title to territory.

It may of course be argued that claims to reparations need not be based primarily on the coercive character of a relationship but on the results held to follow from the relationship. In varying measure, this distinction is drawn by those who press claims for reparations today. Although the coercion exercised in the past by the West over the underdeveloped world continues to be roundly condemned, it is not so much the fact of this coercion that is emphasized in terms of reparations claims as the results commonly held to follow from it. The distinction is important, if only because the argument emphasizing the results of coercion, rather than the fact of coercion itself, appeals to a standard of moral judgment that was laid down by imperialists themselves, liberal and conservative alike. Nor is the argument merely one of emphasizing the benefits that flowed to the West in consequence of its past hegemony over the underdeveloped states. Even more, the argument is one of stressing the injuries presumably suffered by the underdeveloped states as a result of this hegemony. The insistent claim that "you are rich today in large measure because of us" is complemented by the still more insistent claim that "we are poor today in large measure because of you."

On closer inspection, is this distinction between the fact and the results of coercion a distinction without a substantial difference? Clearly, the answer must depend on whether the fact itself creates a strong presumption in favor of the results here imputed to it. It is disingenuous in principle to distinguish force from theft while also insisting in principle that where force is exercised the burden rests upon those who exercised force to prove that they did not steal (and, even more, that where they did not steal they also did not retard the development of those made the objects of coercion). At least it is disingenuous in those situations where "theft," or "retardation," although not made dependent on such protean concepts as exploitation (and its principal ingredient of "equivalence"), invokes an "as if" historical process that we have no reliable way of confirming. There are, of course, specific instances where force did clearly amount to theft. But an immense, and still growing, literature and a decades-old controversy testify that these instances must be regarded as the exception and not the norm.

The objection will be made to these considerations that they suggest the burden of proof must rest upon those who set forth claims of reparations. In fact, they do not do so, though there is no apparent reason why that suggestion should provoke surprise or indignation. After all, claims of reparations are ordinarily considered justified only when they rest upon an established wrong or injury. With respect to the claims set forth by the underdeveloped states, however, the particular injuries alleged have not been established—at least they have not been established in a large number of cases. What is established is simply that the relationships between Western states and most underdeveloped states were once based upon coercion. Reparations claims may be held to follow from this fact. But if they are, they must run the difficulties already noted.

IV

In emphasizing the claims of reparations, I do not intend to suggest that this is the sole moral basis of the claims the new egalitarianism has addressed to the developed states. To an increasing degree, it is clear that the elites of the new states have moved beyond reparations. The call for a new social contract in which those who played no part in establishing the old order will now participate in the creation of the new is, in many respects, a call that goes well beyond the reparations issue. It is not simply present standards of equity projected onto the past that support the claims of the new egalitarianism. In increasing measure, it is present standards of equity applied to the present and, even more insistently, to a hoped-for future.*

* At the same time, as the following discussion points out, it is also clear that the new order urged by the underdeveloped states does not simply put aside claims rooted

Equality and Justice

These standards, it is essential to observe, are not to be equated with the prevailing response the challenge to international inequality has generated among liberal elites in the West. The conception of social and economic equality entertained by the new egalitarianism differs both in substance and form from the equality entertained by the new political sensibility. To the latter, a just international order requires, first and foremost, the provision of a minimal level of subsistence to all peoples. The categorical justice imperative that arises from the vision of a shared humanity is the obligation to ensure that all persons are granted "course-of-life" needs. That obligation, it is argued, merely responds to the elementary sense of the intrinsic worth of human life and, in consequence, to the desirability of relieving human suffering.*

Even in this apparently restricted sense of needs, uncertainty and controversy will of course arise over what constitutes the minimal subsistence a just order requires. If the answer is given that the duty of minimal subsistence is met when life is sustained, it is obviously open to the objection that the life which is sustained may nevertheless be a life not worth living when all, or nearly all, potentialities for individual development remain foreclosed. If, on the other hand, the duty of minimal subsistence is met only when this objection is overcome, the problem arises for international society of defining the minimum that will go beyond the mere sustaining of life. We know

---

in what are seen as an unjust past. The proposed new order does not proceed on the basis that the historical slate may and should be wiped clean. On the contrary, it is apparent that the equality called for today is one that can be achieved only through measures many of which are in purpose the functional equivalent of reparations.

* The obligation to provide a minimal level of subsistence does not exhaust the new political sensibility. It is, however, the principal obligation that emerges from this view. This point, and it is critical, is often obscured by what are, in effect, emendations of this primary obligation. Thus it is frequently argued that "gross inequalities" of income and wealth are morally unacceptable. But they are morally unacceptable primarily because they exist in a world where many fall below a minimal standard of subsistence. It is the existence of poverty that above all makes "gross inequalities" unacceptable. So, too, the injunction to give what one does not "need" is not merely a condemnation of wastefulness. The duty to give what one does not need presupposes that there are needy and that it is morally unacceptable not to relieve their needs when this may be done without comparable sacrifice by the giver. Of course, this injunction still leaves unresolved the issue of defining those needs that justice requires satisfying.

from domestic experience that there are no readily discernible criteria, certainly no objective criteria, for establishing minimal subsistence in this latter sense. Perhaps the best that can be said is that minimal subsistence is such as will permit individuals to participate in the normal life of their community. As that normal life changes, however, so does minimal subsistence.

Put in somewhat different terms, the postulate of a shared humanity requires that all men, by virtue of their common humanity, be treated alike in certain respects. The difficulty arises in determining those respects in which all individuals are to be treated alike. Unless we are to fall back on the mere sustaining of life, there is no apparent solution to this difficulty, at least none that seems to elicit general agreement. The reason for this is scarcely surprising. What we regard as humane treatment—that is, the treatment men are entitled to by virtue of their humanity—is a standard that will vary from age to age and will reflect the social and economic conditions of society.*

These considerations apart, it is clear that the concept of minimal subsistence, particularly in its broader sense, is addressed primarily to the problem of poverty. When applied to international society, it is a response to the "world poverty" problem. This is the case even though minimal subsistence is linked to development, since the primary purpose of development is not so much to redress inequalities per se as it is to redress certain inequalities, above all the inequalities that are presently expressed by the contrast in consump-

* This is recognized by J. R. Lucas, no sympathizer of contemporary egalitarian currents, who writes: "Whenever inequality results in some people having *too little*, the humanitarian will protest as well as the egalitarian. Human life cannot be properly lived in very straitened circumstances, and we do not show respect for human beings as such if we do not try to alleviate those conditions. Moreover, wealth and poverty are, in part, relative terms: it is not just that there is a certain minimum requirement of food and fuel—true though this is; there is also a varying, and in our age rising, level of normality in each particular community, and to be too far below this will preclude a man from participation in the normal life of that community" ("Against Equality," *Philosophy* 40 [1965]: 302). Lucas notes that the "argument of the rising minimum . . . is by far the most pervasive argument in political thought today. It is a telling argument, but it is open to abuse. It may be a good thing that nobody should be without a television set; but it is only one *desideratum* among many; it does not have . . . the compelling force of the claim that nobody should be without food."

tion standards between affluent and poverty-ridden peoples.* To the degree that this purpose requires the provision of greater equality of opportunity for states, Western liberal elites are willing to make modifications to the present international system. But these modifications, whatever the specific forms they may take, are not to represent basic institutional changes. Above all, they are not to alter in an essential way the market-determined production and distribution of goods. "What must be defended in the large," a recent expression of this outlook reads, "is an economic system which rewards the capitalist virtues of investment, innovation, hard work, and sensitivity to the shifting needs and preferences of consumers. . . . Preservation of the incentives to practice these virtues is essential because without them the world's product will shrink." † The expanded equality of opportunity held out to the South is one that does not threaten a reduction in the prospects for growth in the global product. For it is from this future growth that the underdeveloped states are to benefit along with the developed states, perhaps even to the extent of enjoying a moderately larger share than they presently obtain.

In the new egalitarianism, the provision of a minimal level of sub-

---

* Thus it is not inequality of income as measured in absolute terms that liberal observers have emphasized but inequality of income as measured in relative terms. It is the ratio of incomes rather than the absolute income gap that is found to be of prime significance. In this connection, Karl Deutsch writes: "If human beings are moved mainly by envy, or by the desire to imitate some reference group closely, then absolute income gaps will always tend to provoke indignation and resentment in the relatively poorer country or group, even if both groups or countries should be in fact quite rich, and even if their relative inequality of income should have declined. If, on the contrary, people are motivated mainly by felt needs—that is, by desires for inputs which, if lacking, are followed by observable damage—then these needs should have thresholds of saturation" ("On Inequality and Limited Growth," *International Studies Quarterly* 19 [December 1975]: 391). Deutsch notes that we have little empirical research on which of these responses to inequality might be expected to prevail, though the shape of world politics and the chances for world peace may well hinge on the answer. But the experience within domestic societies provides some guidance in this respect, though it is not very comforting. Some will object to the very manner in which Deutsch delineates these two presumed responses to inequality. Even if "felt needs" are satisfied, it is argued, absolute income gaps—despite a condition of declining relative inequality of income—may be such as to inhibit the realization of equality of opportunity.

† Tom J. Farer, "The United States and the Third World: A Basis For Accommodation," *Foreign Affairs* 54 (October 1975): 93.

sistence is not seen as the overriding imperative of a just international order. Clearly, it is assumed that all peoples are entitled to minimal subsistence. Even so, it is not a humanitarian conception of equality that is made the centerpiece of an equitable international system but the opportunity to participate on an equal footing in this system. It is equality of opportunity that the new states above all demand. May such equality be satisfied simply by modest changes in the present system? On balance, the response of the new egalitarianism would appear to be a negative one. This is so not only because a market system is seen to ignore disparities in economic power and, in consequence, in development. More important is the objection that this system cannot, even with modest modifications, effectively apportion goods in proportion to developmental needs. Instead, it can be expected to perpetuate such inequalities as presently exist. If these inequalities are to be substantially reduced, the reduction can come only through a system that discriminates, and pervasively so, on behalf of the disadvantaged. In this view, equality of opportunity, if it is to be seriously entertained, requires basic institutional changes in the present system and not the ad hoc measures of limited compass currently supported by Western liberal elites.

In this view as well, the significance of meeting humanitarian or "course-of-life" needs appears in a new light. Whereas the new political sensibility in the West finds the primary purpose of minimal subsistence in the alleviation of individual suffering, the new egalitarianism finds the primary purpose of minimal subsistence, to the extent it emphasizes this concept at all, in facilitating conditions of more equal competition among states. In the former case, the obligation is one owed to individuals; in the latter case, it is one owed to states. Nor is this all. In the former case, minimal subsistence is satisfied when the functional needs of individuals are fulfilled. In the latter case, minimal subsistence is satisfied when the competing units are given substantially the same opportunities to compete with one another. These equal opportunities are not met by closing the "protein gap" but by closing the "developmental gap." And to the objection that there is, after all, a connection between the two, the response may be made that there is also a very real difference as well. The filling of the protein gap may be a first, and important, step toward filling the developmental gap. At the same time, given its purpose—or the conception of equality it is designed to serve—it may also prove to be the last step. It is evidently this possibility that the new egalitarianism seeks to preclude through its insistence that a just international order must guarantee equality of opportunity to all states rather than minimal subsistence to all individuals.

If equality of opportunity for states is to be the prime *desideratum* of a just international order, the needs of the disadvantaged that must be satisfied are those permitting fair (equal) competition. Certainly, fair competition cannot take place if some of the competitors are wanting in those conditions necessary for an equal start. Yet the fulfillment of these conditions is not to be confused with fulfillment of the needs that permit minimal subsistence or equality of opportunity for individuals. The principle informing "course-of life" needs is the relief of suffering (or the removal of severe deprivation). The principle informing equal opportunity needs is the provision of an equal start, since without such a start—or, at any rate, its rough approximation—there can be no equal opportunity. The emphasis here is evidently on those inequalities caused by unequal social conditions, past and present, that are presumed to be beyond the control of the disadvantaged—and developing—countries.

It will be apparent that by a different route we are once again brought back to the substance of the issues raised by reparations claims. In principle, there is of course a difference between the duty to make reparations and the duty to facilitate equal opportunity. The former duty arises from wrongful acts and consists in repairing the moral and material damage caused by such acts. The latter duty does not arise, certainly does not necessarily arise, from wrongdoing. The cumulative social conditions that must be equalized, if necessary through discrimination in favor of the disadvantaged, may be viewed as morally neutral (in the sense that no one is held morally responsible for their origins). Even so, the duty to equalize them remains unaffected.

In practice, however, this difference may prove little more than marginal in its significance. At least this would seem to be true once we put aside those natural conditions that have impeded equality of opportunity.* For the discriminatory measures required—or, at any rate, demanded—to equalize cumulative social conditions may well turn out to be substantially the same regardless of whether they are based on the duty of restitution or the duty to facilitate equality of opportunity. Moreover, in either case these measures must elicit substantially similar considerations and provoke very nearly the same controversies. Whether inequalities have been caused by social forces beyond the control of the disadvantaged peoples will depend upon judgments about the past, and for that matter the present, that have already been raised in dealing with claims to reparations. This being so, there is little reason to expect that the difficulties and uncertainties attending reparations claims will somehow be avoided in dealing with claims for equality of opportunity. Instead, what was ostensibly driven out the front door in rejecting reparations claims is largely admitted by the back door in accepting equal opportunity claims. (To so conclude is in no way to reject the latter. It is only to question the persistent view that claims to equal opportunity escape the many problems raised by claims to reparations.)

Whatever the setting in which it may be demanded and the subjects to whom it may be applicable, the demand for equality of opportunity necessarily raises the question: equal opportunity for whom and for what? In the instant case, the answer cannot simply be equal opportunity for development. Although it is true that equal opportunity is demanded by the new egalitarianism in order to develop, it is also true that development is not seen as an end in itself. To some, perhaps many, of the new states, development is an indispensable means for the achievement of domestic social welfare goals. To all, however, development is a means for collective self-realization; that is, for collective power and status. The point, however banal, is nev-

* In the case of collectives, disparities in natural resources, climate, etc.

ertheless obscured by those in the West who no longer regard the state as either a source of value or the indispensable condition of value. Yet the emergence of the new egalitarianism not only reflects the state's universalization consequent upon the decline of empire. It also reflects the triumph of the state in depth; that is, the triumph of the state's persistent claims to men's loyalties. The equal opportunity that is demanded for states reflects the faith with which so many peoples have accepted the state, or the nation-state, as the principal institution for achieving a collective destiny so long denied them.

V

Although the new political sensibility and the new egalitarianism converge in questioning the legitimacy of an international order based on striking disparities of income and wealth, they do so on different grounds and with different purposes. Between the two, it is the new political sensibility that, ironically enough, appears the more radical in outlook and consequence. For the challenge the new egalitarianism has made to the existing order is clearly recognizable as seen from the vantage point of the traditional competition of states. A change in the world's distribution of wealth and power is demanded. It is demanded by states and justified in terms of the equality of states, for the order the new egalitarianism presupposes is an order of states par excellence. It may be argued that the "real" equality sought on behalf of the collective will ultimately be employed primarily on behalf of individual goals, that national self-fulfillment must be seen to form the precondition for individual self-fulfillment, and that the present emphasis on collective equality is therefore a temporary, though necessary, phase in a historical process whose path will not be dissimilar from the path traced by the more advanced societies. Whatever the merit of this view, for the present and foreseeable future it is not a "shared humanity" as much as a "shared statehood" that will be emphasized. This being so, it is not the disappearance of hierarchy but a challenge to the present hierarchy and, perhaps, the eventual creation of a new hierarchy that is foreshadowed. (Not, of course, in the rhetoric of the new egalitarianism, which foreshadows the passage from an oligarchic international society to one that is democratic and egalitarian. But there is little that is new in such rhetoric. Any good Wilsonian liberal would instantly recognize it.)

However we may assess the outlook and claims of the new egalitarianism, we remain, then, in a familiar world. Not so with the outlook reflected by the new political sensibility. For the essential characteristic of this outlook is not simply its call for an international redistribution of income and wealth but its marked ambivalence toward the state. In contrast to the outlook of the elites of most of the new states, Western liberal elites look increasingly to a global order whose basis is no longer centered exclusively, or even primarily, on the state. Accordingly, the justice imperative that legitimizes order is no longer one that is seen in terms of the interests traditionally entertained by states.

That the justice imperative the new political sensibility proclaims rests in substantial part upon prudential calculations of self-interest is quite clear. Equally clear is the uncertainty that must continue to mark such calculations. We do not and cannot know whether the failure to reduce present global disparities in income and wealth will eventually have the rather threatening, if not apocalyptic, consequences for the developed states that are now almost ritualistically invoked in discussions of international inequality. To the degree that the arguments for reducing disparities in living standards through significant measures of redistribution are based upon prudential grounds, they are almost all open to serious challenge. For nearly all depend on the assumption that the poor states either possess today or will soon possess a marked potential for endangering the peace and prosperity of the affluent states. That assumption, however, is not made more cogent simply by virtue of its reiteration. There has yet to be drawn a scenario that plausibly demonstrates either the potential of the poor or how this potential might be effectively employed. What can be and, indeed, is being plausibly demonstrated are the rising difficulties posed to the affluent by those who clearly are no longer poor yet who remain far from satisfied with their lot. Nor does such interdependence as we have today alter this conclusion. If anything, it serves to confirm it, for the interdependencies that presently form a primary concern of the developed states of the North are interdependencies with those Southern states whose growing wealth—and power—clearly differentiates them from the poor. It is not at all apparent how helping the latter would thereby ease the problems such interdependencies have created. Nor is it apparent how helping the poor would thereby diminish the power aspirations of those whose growing wealth may soon permit them to pursue their aspirations.

These considerations suggest that the new political sensibility is quite likely based upon a mistaken—at the very least, undemonstrated—view of what self-interest requires in today's world. It does not require that the rich must make concessions to the poor because in a confrontation with the poor the rich are, by virtue of their riches, vulnerable in a way the poor are not. The power of the poor that has been made so much of in recent years is either largely a piece of romantic nonsense or—more likely—a reflection of an underlying, if largely unexpressed, conviction that the patrimony of the developed and capitalist states is, after all, hardly worth defending—either because it was largely achieved through the exploitation of others, an exploitation on which its material achievements even now depend, or because the affluence that has been created is itself a form of corruption, particularly in a world where so many remain in or near a condition of poverty, or because material well-being has become an end in itself and, as such, is not only devoid of purpose but ultimately self-destructive. Whereas the first theme is stressed by the radical elites in the West, the other two themes have increasingly become the possession of liberal elites. But if the emphasis is different, the end result may be very nearly the same. For both, it is not the power of the poor that is at issue but the status of an order that either never possessed legitimacy (the radical elites) or is in danger of being shorn of the legitimacy it once enjoyed (the liberal elites).

Even if the prudential considerations on which the new political sensibility rests were persuasive, there would remain the practical difficulties attending its implementation. These difficulties are not resolved, they are merely illuminated, by drawing upon domestic experience. What, for example, does a minimal or adequate level of subsistence mean when applied to international society? At the very least, the determination of this meaning must prove far more complicated than the determination of minimal subsistence within domestic society. Even within the latter, we are by this time painfully aware that such determination continues to provoke widespread and deep disagreement.

Let us assume, however, that the content of the obligation to insure minimal subsistence for all peoples can be determined. Who are the subjects of this responsibility: states or individuals? The answer surely must be states. It is only very infrequently that the proposal is made that resource transfers be shifted from the province of the state to the private individual. And not without reason, for the results of such transference are not difficult to forecast. Thus the principal agents of the obligation to effect the international redistribution required to insure minimal subsistence for all are, and will remain, states. So, too, the bearers of the obligation to effect a greater measure of international "equality of opportunity" are, and will remain, states.

Nor is it easy to see how the bearers of the rights proclaimed by the new political sensibility will be other than states, or governments. This is apparent in the case of such equality of opportunity as the new political sensibility has seen fit to acknowledge. What is less clear is how one may conclude that the right presumably corresponding to the obligation to insure minimal subsistence is a right of states. In theory, of course, it is not, for the responsibility in question is intended as one owed to individuals *qua* individuals. In practice, the matter is bound to be otherwise unless the underdeveloped states concede what they have heretofore shown no disposition to concede. If they persist in this disposition, as may be expected, then any attempt to insure minimal subsistence would have to be undertaken through the medium of the state.

Equality and Justice

The principal burden of these remarks should be clear enough. Whereas the order we have today is an order of states, the justice sought by the new political sensibility is, for the most part, a justice for individuals that can be guaranteed only by the atrophy of the sovereign powers states continue to claim. The ambivalence, even the tension, that marks the new political sensibility is evidently one that centers on the state and its role. For the state is at once the principal instrument through which a hoped-for redistribution is to be effected and the principal obstacle in the way of such redistribution. It is the principal instrument in the absence of effective alternative institutions for redistribution. It is the principal obstacle by virtue of its reluctance to act save on the basis of demonstrable self-interest and its resistance to yield any functions identified with its sovereignty. There is not one concept of order presupposed by the new political sensibility but two, and there is no apparent way by which these quite disparate and often conflicting concepts may be reconciled.

If this essential dilemma inherent in the new political sensibility is given but modest recognition, it is largely because of the conviction that we are entering, or have indeed already entered, a new period in history, a period marked by quantitative as well as qualitative change. Given this conviction, the above dilemma must prove of decreasing relevance, since it evidently presupposes that the international system, together with the states comprising it, remain unchanged in kind. But the new political sensibility presupposes that the international system is being transformed in kind and that this transformation will render marginally significant the obstacles heretofore placed in the way of a global redistribution of income and wealth. For the growing restrictions on the states' traditional freedom of action presumably create the necessary, and even sufficient, condition for the development of an international society that increasingly resembles civil society.

In the vision of a global society entertained by the new political sensibility, the state will remain and still perform many important functions but it will no longer be the state we have known. The transformation wrought by a growing interdependence will eventuate in what might be called the "tamed" state, the state from which the sharp teeth of sovereignty have at last been drawn, and the state in which the parochial interests of the past have been replaced by the planetary interests that the logic of interdependence presumably necessitates. Moreover, the transformation of the state will in turn signal the transformation of man. Indeed, to many who share the outlook described here there is no need to project man's moral transformation; there is only the need to remove the obstacles that impede the transformation already occurring from finding its natural expression. Thus in a recent call for a global redistribution of income and wealth, we read: "It is not because men of good will find it hard to agree on what sorts of things ought to happen in the world. It is because it is so *very* hard to see how to make these things happen in a nationally fractionated system that is politically ill-structured for coping with the world's increasingly dominant needs." * Alter that system by taming the state and the promise of the new political sensibility will become a reality. For then *all* that will be necessary to consummate it, as one writer has observed in words that sum up an entire literature, "is that people in Maine should feel the same degree of responsibility toward the people of Japan or Chile or Indochina as they feel toward California." †

VI

Although regularly defended in terms of an enlightened self-interest, the moral claims of the new political sensibility are not only accorded a central position; their persuasiveness is taken largely for granted by those who share the new outlook. Thus Gunnar Myrdal deems the principle that the world's rich have a duty to share their

* John P. Lewis, "Oil, Other Scarcities, and the Poor Countries," *World Politics* 27 (October 1974): 83.

† Kenneth Boulding, Preface to *World Without Borders* by Lester Brown (New York: Random House, 1972). Boulding adds, "This is pretty small, really, but it is apparently enough to create the United States."

wealth with the world's poor as one that is so apparently compelling it needs no extended defense. So, too, Robert McNamara sees no reason why anyone should seriously question the duty of the developed nations to promote a least minimal equity in the distribution of wealth among nations. And John P. Lewis asserts that for all the world's ideological diversities there is not "a modern social ethic anywhere that could pretend to provide enduring justification for the existing, let alone worsening, inequality in international income distribution." *

This is not the first time that a novel moral position has been so presented. What Myrdal thinks is a necessary truth that needs no defense is, by his own admission, something that was foreign to men's imagination prior to the postwar period. In McNamara's case, a duty he now sees no reason to question is one he is not on record as having been aware of before becoming president of the World Bank. John Lewis' assertion may be true, but even in its narrow truth it is misleading. The material issue is not whether any modern social ethic could pretend to provide enduring justification for existing inequality in international income distribution, but whether there is any modern social ethic that has sought seriously to justify income redistribution beyond the confines of the state. In this regard, it is perhaps significant that the most widely discussed "theory of justice" to appear in the West in many years has scarcely a word to say on the subject.†

Moreover, it is hardly necessary to add that publics in advanced Western countries do not on the whole find the moral claims articulated by the new political sensibility compelling. These claims do not coincide with what continues to represent broadly held intuitive notions about distributive justice as applied to the relations between states. On the contrary, what evidence we have points to the conclusion that the great majority persists in drawing a sharp distinction between the welfare of those who share their particular collective and

* Lewis, "Oil, Other Scarcities," pp. 65, 66.

† A number of critics have emphasized this omission in John Rawls's *A Theory of Justice* (Cambridge: Harvard Univ. Press, 1971).

the welfare of humanity, and to assume that the collective is quite entitled to what its members have created. The distinction does not preclude acts of humanitarian assistance taken in response to both natural and social catastrophes. Even here, however, such assistance is seen to be rendered as a matter of grace or bounty. Although often characterized as a duty, the characterization is misleading in that humanitarian assistance is not given as a matter of duty. In view of the moral freedom enjoyed by the giver, it may just as well be characterized as a right.*

This traditional, and still prevailing, public attitude toward distributive justice in the relations between states may be deplored, but to deplore it is not to explain why it remains so broadly held when it denies what is alleged to be a compelling moral position. Nor will it suffice to argue—as do Myrdal, McNamara, and many others—that this failure to acknowledge the obvious dictates of justice is due to a persisting failure of leadership. For then the question must arise why governments, which are presumably made up of men who are neither extraordinarily stupid and misinformed nor unusually deficient in moral judgment, fail to acknowledge the self-evident and, accordingly, to provide the great publics with the necessary understanding and leadership.

What is of interest here is not the answer a skeptic might be expected to give to this question but the attitude that prompts its being raised in the first place. Why do those who share the new political

* The traditional notion of humanitarian assistance was one involving states. Its occasion was a natural catastrophe of a nonpermanent nature; that is, a flood, earthquake, famine, etc. It is clear from the practice of states that such assistance was rendered as a matter of grace or bounty and not as a duty. Even in theory it does not appear to have been regarded as a duty in the strict or positive sense, as Julius Stone points out in his searching criticism of the *offices d'humanité* notion as developed by the classical writers, particularly Vattel. This is one reason for Stone's insistence on establishing minimal subsistence "as a matter of present duty, rather than of mere bounty," for it is only in this way, he believes, that we can "escape both the wavering indeterminacy of the *offices d'humanité* notion and the impracticality . . . of the restitution notion" (*Approaches to the Notion of International Justice,* pp. 411–15, 450). The new political sensibility, in contrast with the *offices d'humanité* notion, addresses itself to permanent catastrophes—or at least on-going ones—whether natural or social. The duty that arises to relieve these catastrophes is not to be confused with charity or gift-giving. Indeed, in providing for minimal subsistence to all, the rich only give to the poor what is rightfully the latter's.

sensibility simply assume that the case for global distributive justice—at least, to the extent of providing minimal subsistence to all—is so apparent that it scarcely deserves moral argumentation? To some extent, the answer must be found in the conviction, however inarticulate, that the present international distribution of wealth is illegitimate in that it has come about by unjust means; that is, through "exploitation," whether forcible or not. To this extent, the call for distributive justice is indistinguishable from a call for reparations. In the case of the radical elites in the West, the importance of the reparations argument is clear and unmistakable. With respect to liberal elites, however, we can only speculate on its relative significance since it is only seldom directly invoked in support of redistribution. Significantly, even so ardent a critic of the present international system as Gunnar Myrdal draws back from invoking the reparations claim to justify the "collective responsibility" the world's rich ought now to entertain toward the world's poor. Yet the central thrust of an analysis that has persisted for more than a generation, and that has issued in more than a dozen volumes, has been to show that there *is* a strong basis for the claim to reparations by today's poor. If that claim nevertheless remains largely muted with Myrdal, and even more so with others, this is not to say it is without significance.

In part, the answer must be found in a conviction not unrelated to that of reparations, a conviction that is usually given only *sotto voce* expression, when expressed at all. It is the conviction that since the West has forced modernity upon the "backward" peoples, it must bear a responsibility for having done so. Jean-Marie Domenach has put the matter in these terms:

> The Western nations were no doubt wrong in using their cultural superiority as an argument to justify the colonization of "native" populations. The fact remains that they involved these populations in a common undertaking which bears the stamp of historical rationality and technical progress. . . . This being so, the industrialized countries can hardly deny their responsibility towards those for whom they have made it possible, and even obligatory, to follow in their footsteps. Western thought, if it is to remain consistent with itself, must accept the consequences of that universality which it has constantly invoked as a principle.*

* Jean-Marie Domenach, "Our Moral Involvement," p. 126.

In this view it is not so much the specific injustices attending a colonial past that are held to create a present responsibility, but the very act of "cultural aggression" that gives rise to a responsibility toward peoples thereby transformed in consequence of this aggression. For what we call modernization was not only a temptation but a necessity for "native" populations. It was a temptation in that it held out the promise of material improvement. It was a necessity in that it was the only way to obtain independence from and ultimately equality with the West. But surely this is not the only conclusion that may be drawn from the history of Western expansion. It may be argued that insofar as this expansion was a critical agent in effecting the transformation of peoples from being mere objects of history to subjects, no duty arises in consequence of this historical undertaking. Indeed, it may be recalled that it was precisely this transformation that provided the one justification, or extenuation, for Western imperialism by thinkers as diverse as Mill and Marx. Nor is the transformation judged differently by most of the elites of the new states. One may of course still argue the case for reparations on the bases of the methods by which this transformation has been effected. But that is another matter.

In the main, however, it is clear that the answer rests on the assumption of a shared humanity. There is in this assumption nothing novel. What is novel is the insistence that men now act upon this assumption in a manner they have not acted in the past, that they draw positive duties of distributive justice from it that they had not heretofore drawn, and that they give a scope to those duties they have never before been willing to give. The simple, though decisive, claim of the new political sensibility is that we no longer differentiate, *for certain purposes,* between fellow citizens and mankind.

The novelty of the new political sensibility, then, does not consist in the appeal to a standard of justice independent of, and in potential opposition to, the justice of the collective (state). This assumption of a transcendent justice, rooted in a shared humanity, may require that even the "health and strength" of the state do not condone the taking of certain acts that are seen to deny the obligations emanating from a shared humanity. Thus many of the restraints traditionally placed on the just conduct of war have been rooted in the assumption of a shared humanity that cannot be disavowed by belligerents. Though war was permitted by the traditional system for reasons of state, these reasons were not deemed sufficient to justify the commission of such acts of warfare as would dissolve the bonds of humanity common even to belligerents. Those bonds are dissolved, in principle, only when men identify themselves completely with the collective to which they belong and, in consequence, when they believe that the justice of the collective is the only possible justice. In the tradition of the West, at any rate, it has only been on rare occasions that men have admitted, in principle, to this identification.

This being so, it is not the insistence as such upon not differentiating between fellow citizens and mankind that distinguishes the new political sensibility but the insistence upon not doing so for the purpose of insuring that all individuals will enjoy at least a minimal level of subsistence. This duty of providing minimal subsistence to all is indeed novel. Attempts to find it in an earlier liberalism are vain, if only because an earlier liberalism did not stipulate this positive duty even for domestic society. To be sure, the inequalities of income and wealth that liberalism was always ready to sanction were conditioned by the provision that the minimal needs of all must first be met. But these needs were not only interpreted in a quite stringent manner; until this century their provision was not generally considered the proper function of the state. The consolidation of the welfare state is, after all, a post-World War II occurrence.

In the greater society of states, the liberal assumption of a shared humanity found expression in the nineteenth century not in any positive duties of distributive justice but in the duties to promote the freedom of those peoples prepared to exercise their sovereign independence and to undertake the tutelage of those who were not regarded as so prepared. For the latter, comprising much the greater part of Asia and Africa, it was not a redistribution of wealth that liberalism called for but a "redistribution of culture." It is roughly in these senses that we may understand the following words of John

Stuart Mill: "The same superiority of intelligence (which broadens the range of interests), joined to the power of sympathizing with human beings generally, enables him to attach himself to the collective idea of his tribe, his country, or mankind, in such a manner that any act harmful to them, raises his instinct of sympathy, and urges him to resistance." * What is of significance in this statement is not the assumption of mankind's moral unity but the obligations found to follow from this unity. Although Mill assumes a shared humanity, neither he nor those who followed him drew from this assumption what many draw today.†

Nor is this surprising. It is only in this century that disparities in average per capita income between rich and poor countries become striking. Prior to World War I, a large portion of the population of most Western societies lived in conditions we would presently characterize as poverty. The global contrast between affluence and poverty, we need to remind ourselves, is a comparatively recent phenomenon. Even more recent is men's awareness of this contrast.

To these commonplace considerations must be added the further consideration that although liberalism had always held out an egalitarian promise, domestically as well as internationally, this promise was to be realized through the mechanism of the market. Within the state, the free operation of the market would release the energies necessary to create a surplus that, in turn, promised the gradual material improvement of all and even the increasing equalization of conditions. The consolidation of the welfare state responded to

---

* John Stuart Mill, *Utilitarianism,* Everyman's Library (1951), p. 63.

† In the years immediately prior to World War I, perhaps the best statement of liberal ideals is the essay by L. T. Hobhouse, "Liberalism" (New York: Oxford Univ. Press, 1964). Although Hobhouse gives eloquent expression to the belief in a shared humanity, he does not draw from this belief the duties of distributive justice that are drawn today. Instead, such duties are limited to domestic society. The "harmonic" view of society, founded upon common utility, requires: "If it is really just that A should be superior to B in wealth or power or position, it is only because when the good of all concerned is considered, among whom B is one, it turns out that there is a net gain in the arrangement as compared with any alternative that we can devise." Hobhouse's formulation is a weaker version of John Rawls's difference principle— also confined to domestic society—in that the latter requires that social and economic inequalities are "to the greatest benefit of the least advantaged."

circumstances in which scarcity was overcome, yet the distributive mechanism of the market failed to operate as expected. Once the earlier premises of liberalism had been modified domestically to allow for the welfare state, the question arose whether these premises could remain unchanged in their application to international society. And it arose at a time when the extension of legal and political equality to formerly dependent peoples coincided with the emergence of global disparities of income and wealth that could no longer be ignored.

Whatever the inherently egalitarian logic of liberalism, then, that logic depended for its unfolding on circumstances that materialized only in the years following World War II. As on an earlier occasion, when liberals discovered the contradiction between championing liberty at home while continuing to suppress it abroad, they now discovered the contradiction between providing for minimal subsistence at home while disavowing the duty to insure such subsistence abroad. On both occasions, these discoveries were prompted in no small degree by pressures of the disaffected. Moreover, in the insistence upon realizing a global welfare community there is more than a trace of disillusionment on the part of Western liberals with what their own societies have wrought. The cause of the world's downtrodden is not simply an essay in altruism, nor a response to prudential calculations of self-interest, but a means of expressing distaste and hostility toward societies from which a substantial portion of liberal elites is increasingly estranged—though for reasons that remain, after much speculation, unclear.

VII

It does not seriously detract from the novelty of the claim that we no longer differentiate, for certain purposes, between fellow citizens and mankind, to point out that its content is in many respects unclear. Nevertheless, it is so even in the elementary sense that it leaves uncertain what *is* the inequality that cannot be justified. Presumably, this inequality pertains to individuals and not to collectives (or, to the extent it pertains to collectives, it still does so only to satisfy individual standards of welfare). In addition, it presumably does not content itself simply with meeting the individual's barest physiological needs—that is, with such food, fuel, shelter, and medical care as are necessary to maintain existence—but with ensuring a minimal or adequate level of subsistence to all.* We have earlier remarked on the difficulties inherent in taking this concept from its domestic context and attempting to give it satisfactory meaning in a global setting. One difficulty is that there is no "normal life" of international society that is comparable to the normal life of a domestic society. (Does this mean, as seems not unreasonable to infer, that within the same scheme of justice a variable sense of deprivation will be understood to permit variable meanings given to a "normal life," thus permitting in turn considerable disparities in international income distribution?) Another difficulty arises from the consideration that in Western countries (and clearly in the United States) the goal of minimal subsistence, such as will enable the individual to participate in the normal life of the community, is increasingly equated with the goal of equal opportunity. Indeed, the purpose of minimal or adequate subsistence is largely seen in terms of insuring equal opportunity. But if this is so, then the meaning of "equality of opportunity" can be no more apparent in the context of international society than the meaning of a "normal life." If the absence of roughly comparable levels of development renders obscure the meaning of a normal life, this absence must render similarly, if not more, obscure the meaning of equality of opportunity.

* There are, as noted earlier, other formulations of the inequality that cannot be justified and, in consequence, of the duty to remedy such inequality. But apart from the duty to give (or give back) to the poor what is theirs—in effect, the duty of restitution or reparation—these formulations appear in the main to be variations of the duty discussed in the text. Thus the duty to give what you do not "need" assumes that a minimal level of subsistence must be assured to all before some may live beyond their needs. How stringent the duty established by the needs doctrine will be depends in part upon the magnitude of the world's surplus wealth and in part upon the definition of needs. The difficulties in defining a standard (or standards) of needs are substantially similar to the difficulties in defining a minimal level (or levels) of subsistence.

Equality and Justice

It is significant that despite the insistence of the new political sensibility that its concern is with individual welfare standards, and that these standards must ensure a minimal subsistence to all, equality of opportunity as applied to individuals receives very little emphasis. This silence may be taken to indicate the belief that in the context of international justice equality of opportunity has no more than a limited relevance to individuals, because the equalization of opportunity for individuals remains within the purview of domestic justice. On this matter there is no substantial divergence between the new political sensibility and the new egalitarianism, though the former draws a connection between the provision of minimal subsistence to all and the progressive realization of individual equality of opportunity within a given community. In the main, then, equality of opportunity is relevant, in the context of international justice, to the collective. In the new egalitarianism, the demand for applying equality of opportunity to collectives is, as we have seen, critical. And although it is much less significant to the new political sensibility, here too its relevance to a more equitable international order is of course acknowledged.

Yet the meaning and consequences of applying equality of opportunity to collectives are by no means apparent. The meaning of equality of opportunity cannot simply be transposed from its domestic setting to the greater society of states, not only because within its domestic setting it is applied to individuals but also because its application presupposes a given social order. As supporters and critics of the principle alike point out, equality of opportunity is meaningful only within an order whose goals or values enjoy general acceptance to the point of being taken for granted. Unless we assume the society of states constitutes such an order, enjoying a comparable degree of acceptance, the relevance of equality of opportunity must remain limited.

Even if this assumption is made, however, difficulties remain in applying equal opportunity to states. The equal start that is indispensable to the operation of the principle is evidently not satisfied only by the removal of formal inequalities. In addition, there must be

147

the removal of social and material inequalities or the introduction of measures designed to compensate for, or balance out, such inequalities. In the case of states, then, it is not enough to be rid of unequal treaties and other disadvantages associated with formal inequality. One must also compensate for such social and material inequalities as will otherwise inhibit equality of opportunity. How does one do this, however, for collectives at very different levels of development? We do not have here the prospect of providing an equal start, as it were, with each new life or with each new generation. The collective is not "renewed" as is the individual, and differences in levels of development may not be overcome save over long periods. Even in the case of groups within domestic society, it has been argued that these same conditions of social and material inequality, persisting over long periods and also resulting in different "levels of development," must frustrate attempts to apply the principle of equality of opportunity. The case for discrimination in favor of racial minorities has been made on these grounds. Does the new political sensibility join with the new egalitarianism in making a similar case for the poor countries? We have earlier concluded that it probably does not do so. If it does, the way is opened in the case of the poor states for discriminating on their behalf. But how much discrimination? The answer, once again, remains unclear.*

Then, too, there is the question already raised in a different context: to what ends will states employ equality of opportunity? The

* Together with a growing number, Seyom Brown in *New Forces in World Politics* (Washington: The Brookings Institution, 1974), p. 206, suggests that the task of specifying criteria of distributive justice might be clarified by applying John Rawls's difference principle requiring inequalities to operate to the greatest benefit of the least advantaged. It is not clear, however, whether this principle would be satisfied by decreasing *relative* differences in average per capita income or whether it would require a decrease in *absolute* differences as well. If only the former differences need be reduced, then the difference principle is compatible with existing, and even increasing, absolute income gaps. Similar uncertainty attends the attempt to apply Rawls' conception of equality of opportunity in the instant case. Not that Rawls is opposed to discriminating on behalf of the disadvantaged in the name of equal opportunity. On the contrary, he writes (p. 303) that "an inequality of opportunity must enhance the opportunities of those with the lesser opportunity," a rather convoluted way of saying that discrimination is justified when undertaken on behalf of the disadvantaged. But how much discrimination? The answer remains unclear.

question is only infrequently raised, whether by Western liberal observers or by spokesmen of the new states. Does this silence indicate the belief that equality of opportunity will be sought within an order whose goals or values enjoy general acceptance? If it does, one would like to know the basis for such a belief. Certainly, it will not do to argue that equality of opportunity will be sought only for domestic consumption and welfare goals. In part, equality of opportunity will be sought for these ends. In part, however, it will be sought for the purposes of collective power and status; that is, for purposes that are essentially competitive in character.

It is quite true that within domestic society the purposes for which equality of opportunity is sought may also be competitive in character. But there is a world of difference between the competition for power and status within most domestic societies affording scope for equal opportunity and the competition for power and status within international society. The attempt to assimilate the latter to the former, for the purpose of evaluating the consequences of equal opportunity as applied to international society, must ignore the obvious differences between the two "societies." Within domestic society, the operation of equality of opportunity does not place the losers in the struggle at a fatal disadvantage. (This includes the "losers" on both ends of the economic and social spectrum. The prevailing assumption has been that although the new beneficiaries of equality of opportunity would find their position improved, this improvement would not take place at *marked* cost to those who already enjoyed a preferred position. Moreover, on balance this assumption has been borne out by experience. Typically, in domestic society the result of equality of opportunity has been upward social mobility.) In international society, the consequences of implementing equal opportunity are of necessity far more speculative and hazardous. This is one reason why states enjoying a privileged position have regularly opposed equality of opportunity. And not without reason, since the consequences of equal opportunity cannot be judged apart from the society in which it is intended to operate. In a society marked by the absence of effective collective procedures and lacking in commitment to a common good, it is vain to pretend that these consequences need not be feared by those whose power position might suffer in consequence of implementing the equal opportunity principle.

These considerations need not be extended. Despite the failure to clarify what *is* the inequality that cannot be justified, this failure may be seen as much less significant than the insistence upon realizing a new pattern of distributive justice, though one presently undefined, that no longer draws a distinction in principle between fellow citizen and mankind. What is the argument made for regarding as morally unacceptable today a distinction that has heretofore been viewed with moral equanimity, if not indifference?

In part, of course, the answer is to be found in the postulate of a shared humanity, in the argument that we ought to treat all human beings with the respect to which they are entitled by virtue of their humanity. Enough has been said to indicate that the principle of shared humanity may be given, and has been given, a greatly varying content, that the obligations held to follow from the universal common humanity of men are anything but self-evident (since the critical issue of the respects in which men must be treated similarly by virtue of their humanity is left open), and that in consequence the argument of a shared humanity may be used to effect not only so-called humanitarian ends but broadly egalitarian ends as well. The shared humanity postulate need not take—and, if faithfully interpreted, should not take—account of proximity, distance, or whether the persons to be accorded the respect due them by virtue of their humanity are related to the actor by any scheme of social cooperation (interdependence). There are, in brief, no circumstances—real or imagined— that condition the obligations held to follow from a shared humanity save the circumstance (fact), imminent in the very formulation of the principle, that all men, being men, share a common humanity.

It is this very simplicity, though, that is also a source of weakness. In rejecting the moral relevance of proximity, distance, or—most critically—social grouping, the argument of a shared humanity rejects if not human nature then human history. It assumes the capacity of sympathetic attachment to those with whom the only tie is—or may be—a shared humanity, whereas a uniform experience indicates that the internalization of the sense of obligation to sacrifice for the welfare of others depends if not upon proximity then upon discrete and identifiable social grouping. For better or worse, the nation-state has been the largest social grouping able to command such sacrifice.*

The new political sensibility does not on the whole reject this experience and the lesson it conveys. Although emphasizing a shared humanity, it appears that the primary purpose of this emphasis is to establish the content of duty—the inequality that cannot be justified—rather than the source of duty itself. The minimal subsistence that is due to all is justified in terms of a shared humanity. But the obligation to act upon a shared humanity is in turn made dependent upon the prior obligation that follows from the fact of community and is indeed coincidental with it. What establishes a community, though, is not the state; rather, it is the preexistence of community that makes possible the liberal state. In this view, then, the state is the superstructure of community, and though the superstructure is important, it is not to be confused with the underlying reality of community. Nor may it be accorded the same value as the community, for the justification of the state is ultimately no more, though it may be much less, than the justification of the community. But the community is, in turn, nothing other than the individuals who comprise it and who are related to one another by a certain mutuality and intensity of interest. It is this mutuality and intensity of interest, manifested in the main by a variety of economic and social relationships, that transforms the concept of a shared humanity from a noble aspiration, though one without practical consequence, into a positive duty to provide minimal subsistence to the world's peoples without regard for national boundaries.†

* "For better or worse" because here, as elsewhere, the state is Janus-faced. If "progress" in morality is defined as the extension of the sense of sympathy to ever larger human groups, the state, or nation-state, must be seen as at once the great instrument of moral progress and the great impediment to such progress.

† Strictly speaking, there is no reason why the content of duty should be held to that of providing minimal subsistence. If the world has become, by virtue of a growing

Whatever one may think of this argument, there seems little question but that it is the essential argument underlying the new political sensibility. It is men's interdependence, rather than their common membership in the state, that is taken as constitutive not only of order but of justice as well. If this essential truth has been obscured, it is because the history of humanity to the present period has in fact been a history of communities that, though related in varying degree, nevertheless could and did maintain a discrete existence. Given this condition, obligation was expectedly coincidental with the state, since the state was coincidental with community. Moreover, being coincidental with community, and serving effectively on the whole to protect the interests of community, the state came to be seen if not as the source of value (hence of obligation) then as the indispensable condition of value. But the historic circumstances that made the state coincidental with community and that allowed the state to be seen as the indispensable condition of value expressed no permanent truth. In a period when this coincidence no longer obtains, when the inter-

---

interdependence, one vast economic and social system, justice may be seen to require that the disadvantaged enjoy a still more favorable sharing of the benefits derived from interdependence. We have specified those benefits in terms of minimal subsistence because the new political sensibility so specifies them and because the very open-endedness of minimal subsistence would have, if seriously implemented as a principle of global distributive justice, quite radical consequences. Indeed, in view of the open-ended quality of minimal subsistence, it is not easy to conceive what a still more favorable sharing of the benefits derived from interdependence might be—at least within the limits of what is economically feasible today. If this is true, then the efforts of many to apply the Rawlsian theory of justice to the world appear rather superfluous, since application of the difference principle could scarcely achieve more radical results than application of the principle of minimal subsistence. It is another matter to criticize Rawls for failing to consider any principle of distributive justice applicable beyond the confines of domestic society. One critical follower points out that Rawls's failure to extend his theory of justice beyond the confines of domestic society rests on an assumption (self-sufficiency) that "is not justified by the facts of contemporary international relations. The state-centered image of the world has lost its normative relevance because of the rise of global economic interdependence. Hence, principles of distributive justice must apply in the first instance to the world as a whole, then derivatively to nation-states" (Charles R. Beitz, "Justice and International Relations," *Philosophy and Public Affairs* 4 [1975]: 383). Beitz's position draws added strength from his assertion that interdependence is a pattern of relationships imposed on the poor and weaker states and one whose benefits are very largely one-sided. Even so, the obligations of distributive justice would hold whatever the precise assessment made of the present operation of interdependence.

ests that comprise community transcend the state and, in consequence, can no longer be guaranteed by it, what was once an indispensable condition of value is readily transformed into the principal impediment to value.

There is no difficulty, then, in answering the question why those who share the new political sensibility assume that the case for a global distributive justice is apparent. They do so because they consider such interdependence as exists in today's world as constitutive not only of order but of justice as well. And if one—indeed, *the*—essential ingredient of that justice is a greater measure of equality, it is presumably because an interdependence that cannot be avoided save at prohibitive cost also cannot be expected to function without substantial reduction in present disparities of global income and wealth. It is the commonality of fate imposed by a growing interdependence that creates the need for, while making possible, a greater measure of international equality.

One may of course question the essential premise of this argument as well as its reading of the contemporary scene. There is no need to accept the view that the community makes possible the state. Quite the reverse may be argued, and with considerably greater plausibility. It is the state that, more often than not, has created the degree of interdependence identified with community. Surely it requires a curious reading of the experience of the new states to find in their brief history vindication of the premise that it is only the preexistence of community that makes possible the state. So, too, it requires a curious reading of the international scene to find in a growing interdependence the certain harbinger of the state's decline. Even if we accept the prospect of a world that is increasingly interdependent, the implications of such interdependence as we may reasonably expect hold out as much a threat as a promise (at least, this is so if we do not accept the sanguine view that interdependence is itself constitutive of order). Is it reasonable to expect that governments and publics will embrace the promise while refusing to resist the threat? If not, one may find in interdependence a precise reason for governments eventually intent on increasing the powers of the state.

In a way, the new political sensibility also acknowledges the possibility, and even the desirability, of a world in which states, far from declining, will instead grow in the powers they yield. This is the expectation, at least, with respect to the underdeveloped countries, for the Herculean task of development is not viewed as one that can be readily undertaken by weak governments. But the prospect of strong governments in the new states presents problems. Will these countries be receptive to transfers of resources from the rich states that are intended to reduce individual income distribution not only as between rich and poor countries but within the poor countries as well? We do not seriously raise here the condition that such transfers be also designed to promote the growth of fundamental personal freedoms, for the new political sensibility shows little apparent interest in this. It is the persistence of material disparities that commands primary attention rather than the persisting denial of personal freedoms, despite the fact that the latter may surely be included in the proposition of a shared humanity.

Clearly, the new political sensibility is oriented toward equality, not liberty, at any rate in the sense that if a choice must be made between liberty and the reduction of material inequality it will be made in favor of the latter. This preference should be recognized for what it is and not obscured by specious arguments attempting to show that, after all, in the circumstances of most underdeveloped states the choice itself is meaningless (or an illusion), or that personal freedoms will be the consequence of an improved standard of living (which may or may not be the case), or that personal freedoms can only be guaranteed by measures of intervention in the domestic affairs of states (which may be true but if so is equally applicable to attempts to insure internal equity of income distribution). Although the preference for equality in the case of the poor countries is not compelling, it is surely a plausible and, in many cases, even a persuasive position. But nothing is gained by the political claptrap that regularly justifies this preference on the part of Western elites.

Still, how does one insure the proper conditions for the realization of greater internal equality? Although the equality that the new political sensibility places so high a premium on is the equality of individuals, this equality must still be achieved through the medium of states. Accepting the view that international redistribution must be determined above all by the criterion of need—that it is the needy rather than the efficient or the good who have a prior claim to the resources of the developed states—the problem remains of insuring that the needy will be served. On this critical issue, what otherwise appears as an impressive consensus begins to fall apart. To some there is no way of insuring internal equity without setting political conditions for the recipient government that will almost surely prove unacceptable because these conditions touch the nerve root of its domestic order. In doing so, they must also strike at the equality of state doctrine. There is thus a potential, and in practice a growing, conflict between the goal of individual equality, sought by Western elites, and the goal of collective equality, prized above all by elites of the new states. A McNamara draws the conclusion from this conflict that the developed states, and of course international agencies, are limited to mere exhortation. A Myrdal draws the conclusion that governments refusing to address themselves to correcting internal inequities should be denied outside assistance, no matter how needy their populations. Myrdal's position is one of aid with political conditions, and stringent political conditions at that. Even so, there is no more than a marginal prospect that such transfers of resources as we are likely to see in the near future will be attended by more than exhortation to the developing states. Whatever the pretensions of the new political sensibility, the rights of the "needy" will, in practice, remain first and foremost the rights of states and not of individuals.

VIII

There is no need to provide more than the barest summary of the contrasting outlooks examined in these pages. The point has been made time and again that in dealing with the new egalitarianism we remain in a familiar world. The claims put forth by the elites of the new states leave little room for doubt or speculation; they are as old as the state system. When stripped of their rhetorical trappings, they call for a redistribution of wealth and power, a redistribution that is to be sought through the state and for purposes determined by the state. It is an old game, placed in a new and vastly expanded setting and carried on by partly different means, but an old game nonetheless. With the new political sensibility, however, we find ourselves in a world whose nature we can only partially discern. For the game we are asked to play here does appear new, whether it is seen from the vantage point of the players themselves or in terms of the interests for which the game is presumably to be played.

It is the very familiarity of the new egalitarianism that enables the observer to project its future with a reasonable degree of assurance. Unless one indulges the assumption that the new states indeed represent something new, their future behavior will not be determined indefinitely by their common past. For some time yet, this past may be expected to preserve a measure of solidarity. But such solidarity may not be expected to persist in the face of growing disparities of wealth and power among the new states and the attending differences in interest these disparities bring.

It is another matter entirely to speculate on the future of the new political sensibility. Will the new outlook continue to be held by those who presently subscribe to it and, if so, will its influence gradually spread to governments and publics? To attempt an answer even to the first question seems very difficult, if only because we are dealing with a view that is held with varying intensity and with varying motivation. The common root of the new sensibility is the proposition of interdependence. But interdependence may still be seen to convey quite different lessons, To some, it conveys the lesson that though the methods of the old politics must be changed, the interests of the old politics remain essentially unchanged. In this sense, the politics of interdependence is a new way of having one's way, and the new political sensibility is an ingenious—or artfully disingenuous—rationalization for what remains an imperial policy that makes such concessions as appear necessary to placate and, hopefully, to co-opt the disaffected.

If this is not an unfair characterization of some who subscribe to the new political sensibility, such subscription may still prove significant. It is easy enough to say that should the price entailed by the politics of interdependence become too great, it may always be abandoned along with the new outlook that serves as its ideological handmaiden. At the same time, there may be a substantial price to pay in abandoning methods to which one has become increasingly committed in act as well as in word. Those who have assumed that they could always "manage" interdependence in such a way as to serve their particular interests might find that in large measure they have instead become the managed. It would not be the first time this has happened. At any rate, even if harshly criticized by some as hypocrisy, the new political sensibility may yet prove significant when we recall that on more than one occasion hypocrisy has been the advance wave of a new truth.

In the case of others, there seems no reason to doubt the sincerity of their commitment to the new political sensibility and, in consequence, the substantial sacrifice they would be willing to make in keeping with that commitment. But is it reasonable to foresee that commitment spreading to governments and to publics? John P. Lewis finds it reasonable and occurring through the mechanism of "subversion in high places." "Among nation-state decision-makers," he writes, "loyalties to parochial national interests will be progressively loosened and displaced by furtive, disguised, apologetically held but increasingly insistent loyalties to planetary interests. Actually, such subversion already is rather well advanced. . . ." *

In fact, there is very little evidence to support this projection. The transformation the new political sensibility momentarily expects shows few signs of materializing. There are indications that we are moving, however tortuously, toward the time when governments and

* Lewis, "Oil, Other Scarcities," p. 86.

publics will view limited measures of humanitarian assistance—though not the provision of minimal or adequate subsistence—as a duty rather than as a matter of grace to be taken or not at one's discretion. As measured against the past behavior of collectives, this represents a marked change. And it is through such changes that men progress. Yet it is a far cry from either the collective responsibility called for by the new political sensibility or the claims set forth by the new egalitarianism.

V

The Future of
Inequality

I

WILL INTERNATIONAL SOCIETY become increasingly egalitarian? Are we only at the beginning of a movement toward greater equality that will eventually carry us to the international welfare society many now envisage? Or are there rather sharp limits to the equality we can project, even in principle, without assuming a qualitative transformation of the international system?

These questions cannot be usefully addressed without reminding ourselves of the sources of inequality in international society. The inequality of states stems in the first instance from their varying natural endowments. In a reversal of Rousseau's claim respecting individuals, we may say that political collectives are born unequal and that in consequence of their different natural endowments they are destined to remain unequal. These "natural" inequalities, it is true, have not given rise to uniform consequences; they have not determined in unvarying manner the character of the international hierarchy. The degree to which physical extent, geographic position, natural resources, and population determine collective inequalities of power and status has varied considerably. This is so because the significance of these characteristics depends upon the techniques available in a given period for exploiting them and, of course, upon a collective's capacity and will for doing so. Still, there are limits beyond which natural inequalities cannot be compensated for by states that share the same civilization and a roughly comparable level of development. This has been particularly true of states that have shared industrial civilization.

By far the most striking inequalities that have marked the international system have been those resulting from unevenness of socioeconomic development. It was this unevenness of development that by the late nineteenth century gave rise to disparities of power that had never before been reached yet once reached were to prove shortlived. There are no persuasive reasons for believing that in time inequalities resulting from unevenness of development cannot be narrowed sufficiently to dispel the special sense—and all too often the reality—of vulnerability stemming from the juxtaposition of developed and undeveloped. If an inability to participate in industrial civilization is presently seen by the elites of most of the new states as the critical manifestation of inequality, it is one that will eventually be altered. The attitudes, motivations, and institutions that are so important in determining material progress cannot be acquired overnight. But they can be acquired by elites intent upon achieving a material progress that will insure their recognition as equal participants in industrial civilization.

To what extent are inequalities consequent upon unevenness of development imposed by the international system? And what is the character of these external constraints? These questions have long been a source of controversy. Today, they appear to elicit more controversy than ever. Nor is this surprising, given the failure of reality to conform to the optimistic projections of rapid growth in the Third World that were commonplace until the middle 1960s. Disappointment over the outcome of these earlier projections gave unexpected popularity and considerable persuasiveness to radical analyses of the causes of underdevelopment that stressed the external constraints on development imposed by a capitalist world economy. At the same time, disappointment over the failure of earlier growth projections prompted many Western observers to shift the emphasis they had once placed on the internal impediments to development. Although the record of the developing countries was by no means uniformly poor, it could easily and most reasonably be read to mean that internal obstacles to development—not least of all, those rooted in cultural patterns—would prove much more resistant than had been supposed. But this conclusion was, for a variety of reasons, quite unpalatable. Unwilling to accept the view that the principal constraints on development were still to be found within the backward countries themselves, rather than in the relationships between the latter and the developed states, Western liberals—when not emphasizing population growth—came increasingly to focus their criticism on an international economic system held to exacerbate the plight of the underdeveloped. To these critics, the system could nevertheless be corrected by rather modest reforms that would remove the principal external constraints on development. To the radical critic, the constraints a capitalist world economy places on the developing countries could be removed only with the virtual disappearance of this economy.

There is no need here to review the radical critique. What is necessary to emphasize in the present context is simply the insistence of this critique that a global capitalist economy must be held primarily responsible for the inequalities resulting from unevenness of development. Are these inequalities distinctive to capitalism, however, or would most of them form a part of any international system other than one in which the component units were autarchic (and, accordingly, formed no system at all in the strict sense)? The corollary of the radical thesis that an international capitalist system inevitably produces and sustains the inequalities we find in the present system is that an international economy dominated by socialist states would be free of these inequalities.

The basis for this position is familiar ground. It is contended that the characteristics distinguishing a global capitalist economy would not characterize an international economy dominated by socialist states. Thus the inequalities consequent upon foreign investment would be absent from the latter system. So, too, the inequalities attending trade relations between developed and developing economies would disappear. More generally, and by definition, the needs presumably inherent in and distinctive to capitalist economies—for markets abroad to compensate for inadequate demand at home and for investment outlets to absorb surplus capital—would not characterize an international system presided over by socialist states.

But even if the alleged basic drives of capitalist systems are accepted without question, it is not apparent why wide disparities in development would not also mark a world economy dominated by socialist states. Unless we assume that virtually all significant inequalities due to unevenness of development are the result of external constraints generated and maintained by capitalist systems—a patently absurd assumption—inequalities resulting from internal constraints will persist in a largely socialist system as well. At least they may be expected to persist unless the then-dominant states in the international system attempt to facilitate their disappearance by intervening in the domestic affairs of developing countries. Though ostensibly undertaken for "progressive" ends, such intervention would still be undertaken against the will of governments and very likely of peoples. It may be argued that in an international system dominated by socialist states interventions of this sort would not occur because the circumstances that might occasion intervention would not arise. But there is no more guarantee of this than there is that socialist governments will not arise and persist among developing countries in the present system.

Although there will be differences in the structure of inequality characterizing a system dominated by socialist states, these differences will not be such as to do away with unevenness of development. For an indefinite period, then, it is only reasonable to expect that this form of inequality will persist. This being so, is it also reasonable to expect that all of the consequences presently attendant upon this form of inequality will disappear? Obviously, some will disappear. It is not at all apparent, however, that others will do so. Thus developed states, even though socialist, will still have need to insure access to vital raw materials. The consequences of that need should not prove markedly different from today, unless it is assumed that socialist states would not only consume far less raw materials than capitalist states but, much more importantly, that they would pay a "just" price for these imports rather than a price determined by the market.* The former assumption, even if it is granted, would not necessarily result in the improvement of the position of the suppliers of raw materials to developing countries. On the contrary, it might well worsen their position. The latter assumption presupposes, in effect, the disappearance of the market. But the market determination of the prices of primary goods—indeed, of all goods exchanged—will not disappear simply becuse the international system is dominated by socialist states. What will disappear is the private entrepreneur, his place being taken by the state. A market economy of sorts will nevertheless persist as long as the state system itself persists. If the exchanges between advanced and backward economies are regarded as unequal, largely because of unevenness of development, these exchanges will be unequal whether undertaken within the context of a capitalist or socialist international economy. The difference will be that whereas exchanges occurring within a capitalist international economy may only indirectly involve state interests and power, exchanges occurring within a global economy dominated by socialist states will of necessity directly involve state interests and power.

A predominantly socialist international system would still be a system marked by great inequalities. For an indefinite period it would be a system made up of the rich and the poor. Moreover, to the inequalities consequent upon unevenness of development there would also remain inequalities of wealth and power resulting from varying natural endowments. What are the grounds for believing that this system, in contrast to a capitalist dominated system, would drastically reduce present international inequalities of wealth and power? It will not do to answer by evoking the egalitarian ideal of socialism. For the question is not addressed to the ideal nature of socialism but to the manner in which a socialist society may in fact be expected to behave toward other societies, whether socialist or not. Is it unrea-

---

* A "just" price must be taken here to mean a price that will appear just to both consumers and producers. A price considered just by producers may appear otherwise to consumers, even socialist consumers dealing with socialist producers.

sonable to expect that as long as the international system persists, states—socialist states included—will continue to draw a distinction between their own welfare and the welfare of others? Whether socialist governments will draw a sharp distinction between the welfare of their own and the welfare of others cannot be made to depend upon the extent to which these governments achieve "real" democracy in contrast to the "formal" democracy of liberal-capitalist societies. The responsiveness of governments to the will of the governed tells us nothing about the character of that will. If the governed feel little sense of obligation to those outside the state, a government responsive to the will of the governed has no choice but to act accordingly.

It may be argued that a socialist society cannot act justly at home while acting unjustly abroad, that it cannot be egalitarian in its domestic life while remaining largely indifferent to a world divided between rich and poor. Yet as long as men's sympathy—their capacity for identification—remains bounded by the collective to which they belong, there is every reason to expect that socialist societies as well will draw a distinction between the welfare of their own and the welfare of those to whom they have but a very limited sense of obligation. Nor is this all. The distinction between the (collective) self and others may be quite sharply drawn by socialist governments precisely because the latter will be committed to maintain as high a welfare standard for all as possible. Even if it is assumed that in an international system dominated by socialist states there will be fewer occasions for conflict, this is not to say that there will be no occasions. The causes for conflict between states might diminish, but the remaining causes might still be very significant. Put in other terms, the threshold for conflict might be higher in the new system than in the old. Still, once reached, the resulting conflicts might prove even more serious.

There is, moreover, no reason to restrict the conflicts that may arise in the new system to those rooted in inequalities of income and wealth. There will surely be other inequalities even in a predominantly socialist state system. Not all of these inequalities need provide the occasion for conflict, though some will. As long as the state system itself persists, inequalities of power are likely to constitute, as they have constituted in the past, the prime source of conflict. They are likely to do so not only because security will remain an important concern of governments but because even socialist states may be expected to aspire to influence their external environment, however well-intentioned and progressive their aspirations may be. Given a world that will continue to be marked by great disparities of wealth and power, the occasions for exercising such influence will not be lacking.

A radical analysis refuses to acknowledge these prospects attending a change from a capitalist- to a socialist-dominated international system. It refuses to do so because it assumes that a "humane and democratic" socialism will lead to the transformation of men, to a new beginning in history. That new beginning would remove the constraints of a system that perpetuates unevenness of development. "A socialist transformation of the advanced west," one expression of this view reads, "would not only open to its own peoples the road to unprecedented economic, social and cultural progress, it would at the same time enable the peoples of the underdeveloped countries to overcome rapidly their present condition of poverty and stagnation." * But it is not simply the removal of external constraints that would hold out this prospect for poor countries. Instead, it is the promise that with "a socialist transformation" there would no longer be a significant distinction drawn by the materially favored between their welfare and the welfare of the less favored. The inequalities attending great disparities in development would be rapidly overcome not by—certainly, not primarily by—the abandonment of a system that leaves the disfavored largely to their own devices, even when not inhibiting their progress, but by the emergence of a system in which men's identification with a discrete collective either has disappeared or no longer constitutes a significant limit to the concern felt for those beyond the collective. A socialist transformation of the in-

* Paul A. Baran, *The Political Economy of Growth* (New York: Monthly Review Press, 1957), p. 250.

ternational system would quickly redress the inequalities arising from unevenness of development to the same extent that this transformation in turn heralded the transformation—in effect, the demise—of the international system itself. It is not in an international system dominated by socialist states, but in a transformation of this system into a cohesive society of global compass, that men's sense of sympathy would, at long last, know no boundaries. In the absence of this utopia, the significance of the external constraints placed on development must be found primarily in the state system itself, rather than in the particular social structure of states that dominate this system.

The gradual attenuation of inequalities consequent upon unevenness of development would not alter the collective inequalities of wealth and power that persist among states sharing, nevertheless, a roughly comparable level of material advancement. The latter inequalities are inherent in the state system; they could be removed only by the wholesale recasting of states (so as to make them approximately equal) or by the transformation of international society. Inequalities of wealth and power may be reduced, but disparities of size alone guarantee the persistence of inequalities in collective wealth and power.

A clear distinction must be drawn, then, between inequalities rooted in unevenness of development and inequalities rooted in the very nature of the international system. Similarly, a clear distinction must be drawn between the demand to reduce collective disparities of wealth and power and the demand to alter the consequences such disparities have regularly implied in the past.* The challenge to inequality posed by the new states is most clearly directed against

* These consequences, it is necessary to recall, were such as to render meaningless almost any conception of equality. Thus E. H. Carr's trenchant conclusion on equality in the traditional system: ". . . If we assume that equality of rights or privileges means proportionate, not absolute, equality, we are little advanced so long as there is no recognized criterion for determining the proportion. Nor would even this help us much. The trouble is not that Guatemala's rights and privileges are only proportionately, not absolutely, equal to those of the United States, but that such rights and privileges as Guatemala has are enjoyed only by the good-will of the United States" (*The Twenty Years Crisis* [London: Macmillan, 1939], p. 166).

inequalities, whether real or imagined, rooted in unevenness of development. In lesser degree is it directed against collective disparities per se of wealth and power. Least of all is this challenge directed against the consequences brought about by disparities per se of wealth and power in the traditional system.

Indeed, it may be doubted whether the new egalitarianism is seriously interested at all in altering the consequences that have followed from inequalities inherent in the state system. For these consequences could be substantially changed only by the imposition of severe limitations upon the state's claim to sovereign independence. Yet, as we have repeatedly observed, the new states have clearly placed themselves against such limitations. It is not basic structural change in the system that they seek but a changed position within a system whose structure remains essentially unchanged.* Now as in the past, this system is to be characterized by the absence of effective collective procedures. Accordingly, now as in the past, this system is to be characterized by the "right" of the state to determine when its legitimate interests are threatened or violated and to employ such measures as it may deem necessary to vindicate those interests.

Yet it is the primordial institution of self-help that, along with the "natural" inequalities of states, guarantees that the international system will remain highly oligarchical. The consequences that have so regularly followed from natural inequalities may be sharply altered only if the manner in which these inequalities are employed and the uses to which they may be put by states are also altered. It is the institution of self-help that must be changed if international society is to become increasingly egalitarian. But whereas the decline of self-

---

* Although the meaning given to the term "structure" should be apparent from the discussion in the text, it may be useful to state explicitly that structure denotes here the manner in which power is organized and applied. The distribution, or pattern of distribution, of power, though of obvious significance, is not critical for the determination of structure. Thus the structure of the international system is essentially determined by the fact that the organization and application of power inheres primarily in the state and not in institutions independent of the state. Should that condition change, or even substantially alter, the structure would change and the system would undergo transformation. The same cannot be said, however, of shifts in the distribution of power among states, though such shifts are the epochal events of international relations.

help would signal a markedly more egalitarian international society, it would not necessarily promise a more *orderly* one. The erosion of self-help need not give rise to effective collective procedures. Presumably it would not do so in the absence of what would be the virtual transformation of international society. Nor need the erosion of self-help by attended by those conditions generally providing a stable order within domestic society. In the absence of those conditions that give cohesiveness to domestic society, and that permit order without tyranny, the decline of self-help may only bring increased disorder. For if it is the institution of self-help that makes the "order" of international society difficult to distinguish from anarchy, it is also this institution—together with the natural inequalities of states—that gives international society what order it does possess. The hierarchical character of this society is the indispensable precondition for an order of sorts, defective though that order may be. A more egalitarian international society, though one that continues to lack the institutions characteristic of civil society, also promises to be a more disorderly one than the international society we have generally experienced in the past.*

II

If the above considerations are accepted, it will be apparent that an international system holding the promise of reasonable order and stability can become more egalitarian only within rather closely circumscribed limits. Those who assume otherwise, and refuse to place virtually any limits on the extent to which the challenge to inequality

---

* Kenneth Waltz reminds us of the virtues of inequality by noting that: "In an economy, in a polity, or in the world at large, extreme equality is associated with instability. . . . The presence of social and economic groups, which inevitably will not all be equal, makes for less volatility in society. . . . The inequality of states, though not a guarantee of international stability, at least makes stability possible" ("International Structure, National Force, and the Balance of World Power," *Journal of International Affairs* 21 [1967]: 224).

may ultimately be carried, must also assume something tantamount to the transformation of the international system. If collective disparities of wealth and power, together with the consequences these disparities have had, are no longer to determine the structure of the international system and, in consequence, the limits to equality, it is because the system itself will have been transcended.

Thus to the question, will the international system become increasingly egalitarian, one response is to alter the very sense of the question by projecting a world in which this system will be qualitatively transformed. This is the inescapable meaning of the parallel drawn between the growth of equality within the domestic societies of the West and the greater society of states. If "the world community is bound to become a welfare community, just as the nation state became a welfare state," * it will become so only if the state no longer occupies the role it does today. This is the meaning of those who speak of loyalties to parochial national interests becoming steadily displaced by loyalties to planetary interests, just as it is the meaning of those who find it morally inconsistent to war on poverty at home while remaining passive and indifferent to its depredations abroad. It is not the growing equality of *states* that is foreshadowed by this view but the growing equality of *individuals*. The state may serve—at least, for an interim period—as one institution among others to effect this growing equality of individuals. But it will no longer serve as the principal, let alone the exclusive, guardian of the interests of the human beings who comprise it. As long as it does, there can be no "international welfare community" that is relevant to individuals in a sense analogous to national welfare communities. Nor does this conclusion follow from the inequalities of states. It would hold true whatever the disparities among states, since it is not so much these disparities as it is the continued role of the state in men's lives that precludes the emergence of a world community, welfare or otherwise.

The view that finds a parallel between the growth of equality

* Cf. p. 56.

within domestic societies and international society does not address itself to the fundamental dilemma of a society of states in which the progression of equality is nevertheless marked by the absence of the elementary conditions that have attended, and made possible, the progression of equality within civil society. Since that dilemma remains unresolved, it is not surprising that such equality as exists today in international society remains a structure largely without a foundation. It is only by assuming that this dilemma has been resolved, or very nearly so, that the parallel drawn between the development of equality in the national and international community appears at all plausible. And it is only by assuming that the international system has already been transformed, or very nearly so, that the projection of an increasingly egalitarian global community appears at all plausible.*

A more "moderate" and representative view of the changing character of the international system gives greater plausibility to the prospect of an increasingly egalitarian system, if only because it does *not* project the imminent transformation of the system. This view ac-

---

* The matter is otherwise for those who do not share this sanguine view of the contemporary world, but who are nevertheless persuaded that we are moving toward an international welfare community of sorts. Thus it is one of the difficulties of Julius Stone's position that whereas he is hopeful with respect to the movement toward achieving a global welfare commitment, undergirded by a new sense of "international economic justice," he does not see this change serving "as a sufficient lever for transforming the international 'system' " ("Approaches to the Notion of International Justice," in *Future of International Legal Order, vol. 1,* Falk and Black, eds. [Princeton: Princeton Univ. Press, 1969], pp. 459–60). By this he presumably means that we must look forward not only to the persistence of the paramount role of the state in men's lives but, more to the point, to the persistence of the problem of regulating the use of coercion in state relations. Yet the critical question that arises, then, is this: what are the grounds for believing that although the system will persist, men and states will nevertheless acknowledge a duty toward one another that has only recently been acknowledged within domestic societies (and by no means within all)? The question can be put aside by those who are persuaded that the international system has already changed, at least with respect to the use of force, and that men's loyalties are already transcending the state. Stone clearly does not share this view. It is for this reason that his optimism with respect to an emergent enclave of "international economic justice" is not easily reconciled with his continued skepticism over the prospects for transforming the international system. If that enclave were really to be won, it would signal, in all probability, a degree of solidarity and willingness to sacrifice that in turn would herald the transformation of the system.

knowledges that for the foreseeable future we are destined to live in a world where the principal actors will remain states intent on preserving as much of their traditional independence of action as is possible. This being so, the international system will remain one characterized by self-help, just as the inequalities that will remain of primary importance to the stability of the system will be collective inequalities.

But if the vision of an imminent transformation of international society is set aside, it is clearly not in this view set aside in favor of an "unchanging" society of states. Whereas an international welfare order, with all that this must imply, forms little more than a distant aspiration, the traditional system nevertheless represents a now-abandoned past. Self-help persists in the absence of effective collective procedures, but the scope and significance of self-help, so central to the traditional system, are being steadily and substantially altered. The system remains hierarchical, yet the hierarchy no longer has the salience and the solidity it once had. Although the major states are still the most important repositories of power, the emergence of many new actors—national, transnational, international, and private—no longer permits the state the concentration of power the traditional system permitted.

Nor does this steady diffusion of power permit states, even the major states, to pursue a strategy of independence without paying an ever greater, and even now for most a near prohibitive, price. Instead, the present system increasingly compels states to form relationships of mutual dependence that, once entered into, can normally be broken only at exorbitant cost. These relationships of interdependence, moreover, are for the most part not susceptible to the arbitrament of force. Though interdependencies may and do breed conflicts of interest, the threat or use of force to resolve these conflicts is likely to prove more injurious to the user than non-forcible means (even if the latter should frequently prove quite limited in their effectiveness). Thus the sanctions of the traditional system, the principal expression of which was forcible self-help, no longer respond to the "logic" of the present system. Instead, novel methods of conflict resolution are called for that will respond to a system in which the actors are not only many but of diverse character and the relationships they entertain are at once more numerous, complex, and "compromising" of the state's former independence of action than were the relationships characterizing the traditional system.*

What are we to make of this now familiar view? Does it suggest a system that remains essentially the same despite its many changes? Or does it suggest, notwithstanding its apparent moderation when compared with the view projecting a clear and imminent transformation of international society, that the changes summarized above form the basis for what is likely to prove, after all, a transformation of sorts? The answer is unclear, if only because the view itself is unclear in many respects. Then, too, its expression is regularly attended by qualifications that, if taken seriously, reduce what are initially boldly put forth as radical changes to what are, in the end, quite modest ones. What, for example, are we to make of assertions that although in the "new" system physical coercion has eroded dramatically, if even a very few instances of serious military coercion nevertheless occur the result might well be a return to the traditional system?† Is it particularly enlightening, to take another example, to be told that although the new system implies a new kind of structure, the nature of this structure is neither readily apparent nor, for that matter, need it become so in the foreseeable future?‡

---

* In a vast literature, Stanley Hoffmann has perhaps best articulated the view summarized above. Cf. "Notes on the Elusiveness of Power," *International Journal* 30: (Spring 1975): 183–206.

† (Seyom Brown, "The Changing Essence of Power," *Foreign Affairs* 51 [January 1973]: 294). According to this view, we must act in accordance with the new imperative of pacific interdependence or else we "engender a retrogressive chain-reaction of coercive diplomacy" (p. 294).

‡ Thus Stanley Hoffmann, though asserting that "many more actors, a new type of game [interdependence], also brings with them a new kind of structure," does not delineate the character of the new structure. Instead, he succeeds in increasing skepticism over whether a new structure will emerge to replace the old. "Interdependence may mean a *basic* or ultimate solidarity, but it puts no permanent premium on 'constructive' cooperation. It does not eliminate competition, precisely because the key questions of politics (who commands, who benefits) have not ceased being asked. The fluidity of games without any single minute of truth or clear cut boundaries, played by many players, over many issues allows for multiple strategies" ("Notes on Elusiveness of Power," p. 195). But this is not the description of a new kind of structure. It is, rather, an indication of the absence of any clearly delineated structure.

The Future of Inequality

Still, it is difficult to avoid the conclusion that whatever the ambiguities and qualifications attending the more moderate view of a changing international system, it does project a transformation of sorts. An international system in which national force has become increasingly counterproductive to its users, in which mutual dependencies increasingly limit the freedom of action even of great states, and in which new actors increasingly challenge the once preeminent position of the state may nevertheless be characterized as only a change in degree, not in kind. The characterization is unavoidably suspect, however, if the various changes described are even approximately correct. At the very least, these changes suggest that for the time being we have entered a *systeme mixte:* one that is roughly equidistant from the world we have known and a new world, a new world as yet dimly perceived perhaps but one promising to be radically different from the world of the past. And if the egalitarian consequences of this *systeme mixte* are also difficult to discern, it is apparent that these consequences cannot be circumscribed by the limits imposed by the traditional system. At the very least, the decline in the significance of the state will be attended by the decline in the significance of collective inequalities of wealth and power.

Even a "moderate" transformation of the international system promises, then, a markedly more egalitarian system. It also promises a less orderly system. For the dominant characteristic of the new system will be a decline of power, a decline for which such phrases as the "changing essence" or the "elusiveness" of power are but elegant euphemisms. Power will presumably decline because its heretofore principal form will be increasingly at a discount. At the same time, there is no persuasive reason to believe that economic power will fill the gap left by military power. In some measure, it may do so. But unless the experience of the past proves largely irrelevant to projections of the future, we may expect a system in which the once powerful exercise markedly less control and influence, whether over "others" or over the "system" as a whole.*

* In analyzing the American position within an increasingly interdependent system, Joseph S. Nye distinguishes between the power we may still exercise over "others" and the "erosion of our power to control outcomes in the international sys-

The moderate transformation promises a less orderly system not only because the once dominant form of power will presumably decline, leaving no equivalent substitute, but also because its decline will be attended by the many conflicts of interest that normally mark the relations of states, conflicts that a growing interdependence does not diminish but, if anything, increases. Interdependence increases the potential for conflicts in that it renders the interests of each increasingly vulnerable to the actions of others (though, of course, in varying degree), while failing to provide institutions endowed with sufficient legitimacy to adjudicate effectively between conflicting interests by reference to some larger common good.* Interdependence does not insure that mutually dependent units, because of their mutual dependence, will agree upon a common good. On the contrary, it may only place in sharper relief divergent claims to justice and, in the process, exacerbate these claims while failing to provide the means for resolving them. For the growth of interdependence will be attended by increased awareness among the unequal of their condition. This increased awareness is not likely to be appeased by the argument that when among mutually dependent units all may gain from their mutual dependency all must have, despite their competitiveness and inequality of gain, a transcendent interest in preserving the web of interdependency. The condition of "positive interdependence" is precisely the condition that has so regularly led to revolutionary challenge to social orders marked by great inequalities. It has done so because the gains of the still disadvantaged, though perhaps

---

tem as a whole. The main reason is that the system itself has become more complex. There are more issues, more actors, and less hierarchy. We still have leverage over others, but we have far less leverage over the whole system" ("Independence and Interdependence," *Foreign Policy* 22 [Spring 1976]: 145). The distinction is not an easy one to grasp. Less power over the system has normally been synonymous with less power over others. What appears to be at the bottom of this distinction is simply the conviction that the emerging system of interdependence will prove refractory to the hierarchical ordering of the past. When hierarchy decreases, equality must increase.

* The point is acknowledged by many who remain moderately optimistic over the prospects held out by interdependence. Raymond Vernon writes: "So far as the international economy is concerned, nowhere can one see on the horizon a set of institutions with the legitimacy and power capable of speaking and acting for the collective interests of mankind" ("The Distribution of Power," *Daedalus* 104 [Fall 1975]: 256).

quite substantial by previous standards, create expectations that the principal beneficiaries of a social order are unable or unwilling to satisfy.

In the instant case, moreover, there is evidently no real prospect that an "order of interdependence" will effect a substantial equalization of material conditions. At least, there is no real prospect of this for several generations. The meaning that some read into interdependence may encourage expectations of substantial equalization of material conditions, but these expectations, to the extent that they depend upon interdependence, will remain no more than that. What may be expected is that the resentments and conflicting interests that result from present inequalities of wealth and power will simply go largely unresolved in a system marked by the progressive erosion of the principal traditional institution of order yet without new institutions capable of filling the void.

Thus if the visionaries who see the imminent and radical transformation of the international system hold out the promise of utopia, those who project a "moderate" transformation of the system hold out the promise of growing disorder. The principal basis for order in the traditional system will atrophy. Yet the conflicts that mark the present system will grow, if only because to the conflicts that have always marked the international system must now be added those arising from interdependence as well as from the proliferating demands for an ever greater measure of collective equality. Force will no longer be employed to promote or sustain the formal inequalities of status that characterized the traditional system. At the same time, force will not be employed to promote the realization of collective personality in substantive terms. To achieve the latter, reliance will be placed largely on the politics of interdependence, though the latter is no more constitutive of justice than it is of order. Instead, the politics of interdependence requires, if it is not to degenerate into chaos, a minimal consensus on the principles of distributive justice that will determine the outcomes of the games of interdependence. That consensus, however, is nowhere in sight.

III

It is only on a superficial reading of the challenge to inequality posed by the new states that this challenge is seen to herald a transformation of the international system. The demand for a new and more equitable international order is not to be confused with a change of the system. Instead, it is a demand for a changed position within a system whose essential structure is not only taken for granted but, if anything, highly desired. The outlook of the new states is, with few exceptions, nothing so much as the outlook of those who wish to preserve a system while securing a more independent and advantageous role in its operation. The egalitarianism of the elites of the new states cannot be taken literally. It is not primarily directed against collective inequalities per se, just as it is not directed against the principal institution through which natural inequalities have always been expressed. Accordingly, it is not—and cannot be—directed against the hierarchical character per se of international society but against the particular hierarchical ordering that characterizes the present system.

In contrast to those who project a more egalitarian world by virtue of the transformation of the international system, the elites of the new states project on the whole a more egalitarian system than the present system but one that nevertheless remains unchanged in its essential structure. It remains unchanged because the role and importance of the state remain as central in the system of the future as they were in the system of the past. Indeed, the state is expected to take on an ever greater significance in the new international order. It will do so, if only because the state is looked upon almost everywhere as the principal architect and engineer of development. This is the case even where the conditions for rapid development appear quite favorable. It is all the more true where these conditions appear clearly unfavorable and change, if it is to come at all, must be imposed by governments upon apathetic and perhaps resistant populations. Even in the absence of other circumstances that contribute to the dominant role of the state, and to an emphasis on collective values, the imperative of development is likely to insure that for the indefinite future the state will be regarded as *the* primary source of value in almost all of the developing countries. It is the enhancement of the collective's wealth and power—and status—that must be expected to take clear precedence over the cultivation of individual values.

Given this expectation, it is little more than rhetorical to ask whether the elites of the new states will retain a traditional view of the international system. The demand for a more equitable international system is in no way found to contradict an insistence upon the state's sovereign independence. In turn, the state's sovereign independence—the essence of its equality in both the old system and the "new"—is largely identified with the right of self-help to defend the collective's vital and, of course, legitimate interests. Those restraints on self-help the Southern states have nevertheless championed do not detract from this proposition, for such restraints are transparently designed to deprive the developed states of grounds for intervention against the developing countries and not to restrict the latter in the pursuit of their interests, even if this pursuit must be undertaken by forcible means. The position, common to all the new states, that measures—including forcible measures—of self-help are not illegitimate when taken to vindicate the principle of self-determination, or to liquidate the vestiges of colonialism (which may or may not be consonant with vindicating self-determination), is only the most notorious manifestation of an outlook that affords ample scope for the ancient pursuit of *raison d'état*. Nor, for that matter, is it only against the developed states that these principles may be invoked when interest so requires. They may prove equally useful, as experience has shown, in disputes—territorial and other—arising among the new states themselves.*

---

* The above remarks deserve at least brief elaboration. The possible conflict between vindicating the principle of self-determination and liquidating the vestiges of colonialism arises because what was originally a colonial arrangement may nevertheless come to conform to the wishes of the inhabitants (thus satisfying the principle of self-determination). Even if it should do so, it is regarded as illegitimate by the new states. Martin Wight notes that a limit to the right of self-determination "was that it

A traditional outlook toward the means of statecraft extends as well to the ends for which a new order is sought. Clearly, the end common to the developing countries, whatever their size and natural endowments, is a greater measure of substantive independence, an end to be sought primarily through development. Beyond this, however, their aspirations may be expected to vary in roughly the same manner that the aspirations of states have varied in the past. The small states will entertain the aspirations small states have normally entertained: their security and independence will be given the modest definition that circumstances impose upon them. These states will constitute, as small states have usually constituted, the true egalitarians of the system. In the case of the large countries, by contrast,

---

should not perpetuate a colonial arrangement. Colonial arrangements were, *ex hypothesi*, illegitimate, even illegal'' (''International Legitimacy,'' *International Relations* 4 [May 1972]: 20). If self-determination cannot be invoked in order to maintain ''colonialism,'' then it was only right for Indonesia to seize Portuguese Timor in 1976 without waiting to ascertain the wishes of the inhabitants. So, too, it is right for the non-aligned countries to call, as they insistently do, for the independence of Puerto Rico. The right of self-determination is also limited by the need to preserve the integrity of the new states. This need is expressed in the prevailing principle of international legitimacy which asserts the rights of territorial integrity and majority rule. ''Territorial integrity'' is identified with the boundaries of the state at the time of independence. ''Majority rule'' may be ascertained in a number of ways and need have little, if any, relation to democratic processes. In a survey of the behavior of the new states, Wight concludes: ''The principle *cujus regio ejus religio* was restored in a secular form. The elite who held state power decided the political allegiance of all within their frontiers; the recusant individual might (if he were fortunate) be permitted to emigrate. Minorities had no rights, or only such rights as majorities cared to concede'' (p. 14). The prevailing principle of international legitimacy is presently being tested in Africa. In the case of the Spanish (Western) Sahara, Spain turned over administration of the area to Morocco and Mauritania. With the Spanish departure, however, a liberation movement (Polisario) arose that was backed by Algeria. In justifying their attempt to take over the area, despite the wishes of the inhabitants, Morocco and Mauritania advanced the ingenious argument that recognition of liberation fronts should be extended (in this case, by the Organization of African Unity) only to groups fighting colonial powers, which, by definition, Morocco and Mauritania could not be. The Algerians, on the other hand, have reminded the O.A.U. that if its commitment to the principle of respecting the borders of former colonies should be cast aside in this instance, a dangerous precedent affecting the fate of all African countries would be set. A similar dispute is in progress between Ethiopia and Somalia over the French territory of Afars and Issas on the Horn of Africa. In these and other instances, we find that contemporary principles of international legitimacy afford ample scope for justifying forcible self-help among the new states, despite the norms of the United Nations Charter.

security and independence will take the same protean qualities that large states have given their security and independence in the past. There is no persuasive reason for assuming that the progressive extension of the collective self, which has formed part of the "natural history" of large states, will not similarly characterize the statecraft of the larger among the developing countries. The "equality" the larger and stronger may be expected to seek is the equality the larger and stronger have always sought. It is not the end of hierarchy but the emergence of a new hierarchy that may be projected in the form—initially, at least—of regional hegemonies.

There are many observers, perhaps a majority, who disagree with this summary analysis of the nature and ends of the contemporary challenge to international inequality. But even among those who do not seriously dissent from the analysis there is considerable controversy over the extent of the charge made today—and likely to be made in the medium term future—against the industrial countries by the developing countries. Equally controverted are the prospects held out to the Southern states for achieving the demands addressed primarily to the developed and capitalist states of the West, particularly those demands that go beyond modest and peripheral reforms of the present system (and, in consequence, reforms that leave substantially unchanged the present distribution of wealth and power). Are the more far-reaching and dramatic expressions of the new egalitarianism to be taken at anything even approximating face value, or as merely the rhetorical excesses of a position that on critical examination turns out to be altogether modest in leaving virtually intact the dominant position of the developed and capitalist states? To take the most salient example of the programmatic demands set forth by the developing countries: is the New International Economic Order as outlined in the May 1974 U.N. General Assembly declaration and subsequently elaborated in the December 1974 Charter of Economic Rights and Duties of States to be regarded as expressions of a maximalist position its advocates have no real illusions about achieving? Or are the demands set forth roughly indicative of a position that will not be abandoned even in the face of determined opposition by those who are asked to sacrifice many of the benefits they presently enjoy by virtue of their dominant position? And if these demands are much more than mere posturing on the part of the developing countries, are there meaningful prospects of their realization, even in part?

A decade ago these questions were only seldom raised in the insistent form they are raised today. A decade hence it is possible they will no longer command anywhere near the attention they do at present, even if they are still raised. Enough has been said of those in the West who view the demands of the new states with the utmost seriousness and who believe that if these demands are not substantially met we face the almost certain prospect of an increasingly chaotic and dangerous world. This is, however, not the only response. There is also the view that the contemporary challenge to international inequality has been exaggerated by most of its Western interpreters, that the more sweeping formulations given this challenge in recent years are largely rhetorical and designed to serve internal purposes, and that if the so-called rebellion against inequality does become more than a readily containable demand for marginal change it will be because of a lack of statesmanship on the part of the developed countries—above all, the United States. That a challenge has been made is not disputed. What is disputed are the nature and scope of the *real* challenge (as distinguished from the exaggerated declaratory forms it has taken), the relative strengths and weaknesses of the contestants, the proper strategy to be pursued in containing (or managing) the challenge, and the price entailed by its implementation.

In this view, then, what the principal beneficiaries of the international system are confronted with is a challenge—and, indeed, a need—to reform the present system. Among the demands seriously put forth by the developing countries, almost none is found to suggest systemic change. Whether in the regimes of trade, aid, investment, or monetary reform, what is presumably being demanded would, with few exceptions, result in only modest reforms of the system. For the most part, moreover, the meeting of these demands may be seen to strengthen the present order rather than threaten it. Thus the removal of tariff and nontariff barriers to developing countries' exports would only conform to our professed goal of trade liberalization. So, too, the granting of tariff preferences where such preferences respond to claims of infant industry status would merely accommodate a legitimate need of developing countries at marginal cost to the developed countries. The same may be said for making a positive response to the demand for agreements providing more stable commodity prices, agreements that are consistent with economic growth while meeting the developing countries' need for economic security. In these and other respects, accommodation of the demands of developing states presumably strengthens the system, if only by reducing the grievances of those who otherwise feel they are denied equality of opportunity.

There are, to be sure, demands that are not found "reasonable" in that, if accepted, they would either jeopardize economic growth or promise to effect a redistribution of existing wealth or, finally, threaten to deprive the developed states of their position as guardians of the rules that define the system. In any or all of these contingencies, the vital interests of the industrial democracies would evidently be threatened. Proposals for indexation must therefore be opposed, since their acceptance might well jeopardize economic growth through institutionalizing inflation. Similarly, demands for the recognition of a thinly disguised *right* of expropriation in conditions that are tantamount to confiscation, as well as claims to a *right* to impose exorbitant primary commodity prices through the instrument of producer cartels, cannot be accepted as means of transferring, or redistributing, existing wealth. Nor can the developed and capitalist states permit the control by developing states of those key economic organizations that give institutional expression—whatever the inadequacies of this expression—to the present system.

But these boundaries to the legitimate demands of the developing countries, it is argued, are not only a matter of common agreement among the developed states; claims that push beyond them are largely put forth by the new states as bargaining counters for obtaining much more modest and reasonable reforms that, if granted, would leave the present system quite intact. The demand for indexation and the claim to a right of expropriation virtually without condition are therefore seen as bargaining counters for commodity stabilization agreements and for the exercise of greater control over foreign investment—goals that are no more unreasonable than is the insistence upon greater representation in key international institutions for states comprising some 70 percent of the world population. And to the extent those demands that, if acted upon, would bring systemic change to the present international economic system are seriously put forth by the developing countries, they may be effectively resisted.

The basis for this optimism over turning back "unreasonable" demands is rooted in what are seen as the inherent weaknesses of the developing world, weaknesses that would quickly become apparent in a serious and prolonged confrontation with the developed states. These weaknesses cannot be compensated for by the one trump held by the developing countries; that is, their control over raw materials vital to the Western states and Japan. At least, they cannot be compensated for given the modicum of statesmanship needed to devise and implement a strategy of accommodation. For the weaknesses of the developing countries might be largely overcome only by maintaining a high degree of solidarity both in word and in action. Yet the prospect for realizing such grand solidarity, and preserving it over a substantial period, must be judged very slight given the many disparities of circumstance and interest among the Southern states. If these disparities are nevertheless subordinated to the necessities of a common front, it will only be by virtue of a monumental failure on the part of the dominant industrial powers. Even then, the outcome would probably remain uncertain short of a clear decision on the part of the latter to go their separate ways in dealing with the South.

In the absence of what comes close to a "worse case" analysis, then, the prospects for accommodating the Southern challenge while preserving the present system are considered very strong. Indeed, to the extent there is today a serious challenge posed by the developing countries, it is seen as one that is largely of our creation. It is the obduracy of the principal upholders of the status quo—and above all, the United States—that has brought on the prospect of a serious confrontation by refusing to make concessions that are, quite apart from their intrinsic merit, no more than marginally significant. This refusal to respond to modest demands for change is presumably immeasurably worsened by the inability to accept such change as has occurred. Thus the continued American unwillingness to come to terms with the OPEC countries, particularly its Arab members, leaves these states in a position where they may find themselves with no real alternative to the role of leadership in the Third World. Instead of coming to terms with this "leading edge" of the South, we have chosen a policy of near confrontation. Rather than pursuing a strategy of co-opting the *nouveaux riches,* we have almost by design forced them to pose as liberators of the world's downtrodden.

The means of our deliverance from an unnecessary and unwanted confrontation with the developing countries are therefore apparent. We must begin to distinguish between demands that are not only legitimate by our own standards but imply no more than reforms of a system that remains essentially unimpaired and demands that clearly go beyond the limits of reform (the decisive test of their "reasonableness" or "legitimacy"). To grant the former is not a sign of weakness, as both the Left and the Right would have us believe, but of strength. Once made, the rejection of the latter demands—if they are still pressed with any seriousness—will not prove difficult. For the preponderance of power and advantage will remain with the developed and capitalist states provided only that they retain a basic unity of purpose and action. That basic unity will in part be assured precisely through the grant of reforms that markedly reduce the prospect of serious North-South confrontation. And they will markedly reduce this prospect because they will deprive the South of the most compelling reason for maintaining solidarity. In the absence of this compulsion, the gradual co-operation of the principal Southern beneficiaries of a reformed system becomes not only a viable strategy but one that is very nearly self-implementing.

I V

This, in outline, is the view that has become increasingly attractive to those in the West who reject the projections of growing North-South confrontation—whether of the Left or the Right—yet who also reject the prospect of an emergent global welfare community resulting from the contemporary challenge to inequality. In contrast to a vision that transcends the collective struggle over wealth and power by assuming the transformation of the international system itself, the view considered here finds the challenge to global inequalities one that is made by states and that will be resolved by states. In its identification of the challenge, as in its strategy for dealing with the challenge, the requirements of a realistic statecraft are ostensibly met. At the same time, in prescribing what purports to be a meliorative solution, this view also vindicates its essential liberalism.

Clearly, we have here a view that is in many respects appealing. It is so even if it is neither as realistic nor as meliorative as it claims. Indeed, its meliorative quality must be found largely in the promise to reduce the prospect of inter-state conflict rather than in the promise to improve the wretched conditions of those who comprise a majority of the population of the developing world. It may of course be argued that reducing the prospect of international conflict in which all may lose is itself a meliorative goal. It may be further argued that as long as a state system persists, efforts to improve the conditions of deprived peoples must be undertaken—to the extent they are undertaken at all—through the agency of the state. Whatever the merits of these arguments, the point remains—and it is central—that we are dealing here with a view that is addressed to claims made by states on behalf of states. The reforms urged are those intended to respond to collective inequalities. Even then, the inequalities that evoke a positive response are those designed primarily to placate the elite among the new states. The claims that are to be listened to are the claims of states whose power places them in a position to threaten international stability and, in consequence, the viability of the present system. There is little difficulty in answering the question: who will chiefly benefit from the reforms this view puts forth? The principal beneficiaries are evidently those who already enjoy a substantially increased measure of equality while continuing to insist that the system remains biased to their disadvantage. Greater equality will be accorded to those states that are already well on the way to achieving equality.

The Future of Inequality

Whatever its shortcomings in dealing with the "world poverty" problem and in responding to individual inequalities, does a view that prides itself on its realism indeed respond to the imperatives of power and self-interest? Does it respond even to its initial premise of the deep grievances entertained by the new states? These grievances, usefully termed by one writer the "anticolonialist amalgam," presumably will be satisfied only by the "eradication of all the conditions and insignia of inequality and humiliation associated in the minds of the Southern elites with the epoch of European domination." * Taken at face value, this objective would appear to encompass a great deal. Yet the prospect is held out of accommodating it through what are, after all, quite modest concessions on the part of the privileged nations. Is this not to make trivial those grievances whose depth and intensity we are constantly warned about? If it is not, we must conclude that the recalcitrance of the privileged—above all, the United States—to meet these grievances reflects an obtuseness that is altogether oblivious to elementary considerations of self-interest.

At issue here is of course the question: what do the developing states really want? This question cannot be answered, however, with anything approaching the clarity that many apparently believe. It cannot be so answered because the basic demand of the new states is a demand for a redistribution of power. As such, it does not yield to the rather tidy and modest formulations most Western observers are only too disposed to give it. The "eradication of all the conditions and insignia of inequality" is, in effect, the eradication of dependence. But the eradication of dependence can only come through a redistribution of power. That redistribution will be facilitated by concessions on economic issues. At the same time, such concessions cannot be seen as being somehow isolated and self-contained. They are not sought as ends in themselves but as means for effecting a new structure of power that, like all structures of power, possesses an economic as well as a military dimension. This being the case, there is no apparent reason for assuming that the new states will be satis-

* Tom J. Farer, "The United States and the Third World: A Basis for Accommodation," *Foreign Affairs* 54 (October 1975): 79.

fied by what are little more than marginal changes in the present order. Nor is it apparent why they should be satisfied with such changes if the result is to leave them—if only in their eyes—substantially dependent upon the principal custodians of the present order.

These considerations need not be read as support for a policy of resisting concessions, however modest, to the South. An accommodationist policy that follows the general lines sketched above may well be the course of wisdom for those who are asked to do the accommodating. If it is, however, it is not because those calling for change are asking for so little. Instead, it is presumably because those calling for change can exact a heavy price if such change is not granted, a price that is disproportionate in its cost to the price of change. There is something inherently implausible in the commonly voiced charge that although the new states want so little, we will nevertheless not grant them what little they want. We will not do so, moreover, though the price for not doing so must prove quite disproportionate to what we were asked to concede. The argument is implausible not because it assumes greed but because it assumes that we have magnified—indeed, created—a conflict that easily might have been avoided by the minimal display of enlightened self-interest.

It is another matter entirely to argue that although the conflict arising from the demand for a redistribution of power is deep-rooted, it may nevertheless be contained through a strategy that combines firmness with a willingness to accommodate. The reality of the conflict is not spirited away by the assumption, however inarticulate, of an underlying harmony of interests between defenders of and challengers to the status quo. The seriousness of the grievances entertained, as well as the scope of the demands made, by the new states is not in effect denied by the insistence that only marginal issues are at stake. As long as these assumptions are held to, it is difficult to understand why the prospect of North-South conflict should occasion serious concern. Even if they are dropped, though, is there still reason for finding in an accommodationist strategy the means of our deliverance from the prospect of serious confrontation?

The Future of Inequality

In large measure, the answer is seen to turn on the effects an accommodationist strategy is expected to have in eroding the ties that to date have preserved a residual measure of solidarity among the developing countries. Indeed, the issue of Southern solidarity is commonly regarded as *the* issue that must be addressed above all others. For the promise of an accommodationist strategy is to be found primarily in the success it is expected to have in co-opting the elite of the Southern states into the present—though, of course, reformed—system. Co-optation necessarily assumes that the ties rooted in a shared past will yield to more rational calculations of self-interest, that the inducements held out to the favored few among the new states will soon be found to outweigh the sympathetic involvement that reflects the "anticolonialist amalgam." But if the memories and grievances forming this amalgam are anywhere near as strong as many apparently believe, it will not prove easy to break bonds forged by a common past. Certainly, the prospects for doing so appear slight if the means are limited to modest gestures on the political level and equally modest reforms of the international economy. Moreover, as one shrewd observer of North-South relations notes, what appears as "irrational" behavior of Southern states may nevertheless be expected to last "as long as it is *perceived as rational* behavior by its practitioners. The period is likely to vary with each issue and with the environmental factors encompassing each negotiation." *

Will this perception become increasingly artificial and difficult to sustain, given the increasing heterogeneity of the Southern states? Will growing disparities in wealth and power and, of course, the ambitions and interests that attend rising power strain beyond endurance even a residual Southern solidarity? The answer remains unclear. It remains so even if confined within the bounds of conventional calculations of state interest. No doubt, the disparities that increasingly mark the respective positions of the developing countries will be, and indeed even now are, reflected in the divergent interests enter-

* Roger D. Hansen, "The Political Economy of North-South Relations: How Much Change," *International Organization* 29 (Fall 1975): 930.

tained by these countries. It is another matter, however, to conclude from this that the capacity for meaningful confrontation with the developed states must virtually disappear—at any rate, in every sense save the purely rhetorical. For the cohesiveness of the new states in confronting the developed countries is not in the first place a function of their similarity of interests in general but of their similarity of interests with respect to the developed countries. And even this way of putting the matter may overstate the basis required for cohesiveness in confronting the developed countries, since it suggests that this basis is a similarity of interests that, though it may not obtain in many instances, is not really needed. Instead, all that must be shown is that the abandonment of solidarity holds out little if any promise of gains in excess of the losses—however modest—resulting from desertion of a common position.*

The example afforded to date by the events resulting from the actions of the oil-producing countries of OPEC illustrates the point at hand. What accounts for the support given OPEC by those among the developing countries—middle income and poor alike—that have suffered from the actions of the oil-producing countries? Many have pointed to the motives of fear and hope—fear that open hostility to OPEC would invite retaliation and hope that support would bring relief in the form of OPEC aid to those seriously affected by increased oil prices. In fact, it is now apparent that the aid programs of the OPEC countries will not in any significant manner relieve the distress caused to most non-oil developing countries by the rise in oil prices.† If hope is vain for many, fear also appears largely unwarran-

---

* The argument in the text may be put too baldly. It assumes a degree of rationality in the calculation of interests that may prove unwarranted. Even if the abandonment of solidarity holds out little promise of positive gain, some may nevertheless take this course whether out of a sense of frustration or, more likely, out of a sense of relative deprivation. Then, too, the solidarity of the developing countries need not be seen to preclude divisions arising among them. A broader consensus in confronting the developed states may well be attended by conflict over the strategy of confrontation and, of course, the distribution of the respective gains and perhaps losses resulting from confrontation. In a word, cooperation may be expected, here as elsewhere, to coexist with conflict; the larger game does not preclude smaller games.

† For a recent and careful survey of aid programs of OPEC countries cf. Maurice J. Williams, "The Aid Programs of the OPEC Countries," *Foreign Affairs* 54 (January

ted, since it is difficult to see what measures of retaliation might be taken by the OPEC countries against those who refuse to support the oil producers. The latter, it is true, might respond to rising opposition of other non-oil developing countries by abandoning their role as the vanguard of Third World demands. But this step would also pose certain risks for the OPEC countries in that it would deprive them of whatever domestic support, and international legitimacy, they receive from their present ties with the other developing countries.*

In a broader context, it may still be argued that OPEC support in the Third World does largely stem from a mixture of hope and fear. The hope is that OPEC will not only serve as a model others may emulate but that the oil producing countries will eventually succeed in wringing various concessions from the developed states that will generally benefit the position of the developing countries. The fear is that the co-option of OPEC—or, at least, of the major producers—by the North would leave many remaining Southern states as dependent and powerless as ever. These broader considerations are undoubtedly at work. At the same time, what gives them particular force and persuasiveness is the simple conviction that there is nothing to be gained by abandoning a position of common support for OPEC. Clearly, it is not enough to remind the non-oil producing countries of the distress that higher oil prices have caused them if the altogether likely prospect is that this distress will remain essentially unchanged after breaking with OPEC.

1976):308ff. Williams confirms what others have surmised: that OPEC aid is heavily concentrated on a very few recipients.

* The risks the OPEC countries would run if no longer supported by other developing countries may be questioned. Certainly, these risks vary from state to state. Hansen (*op. cit.*, p. 942) notes that: "For some of the smallest and richest, the threats are likely to originate from outside their borders and may come in such disparate forms as a radically-oriented struggle for Arab unity or straightforward regional hierarchical struggles. For other OPEC states, the dangers may take the form of radical domestic political challenges to leadership which appear to be joining the 'old rich' of the world too rapidly." It is difficult to assess the significance the OPEC countries place simply on the diplomatic support of their position by other developing states. Probably a good deal less significance is read into this support today than in 1974, when the acquiescence of the West to the actions of the oil cartel was in doubt. It is apparent that some significance is still attributed to continued support by non-oil developing countries.

A not dissimilar reasoning applies to the calculations of the OPEC countries. What do they stand to gain by abandoning their chosen position as champions of the developing world? Is the promise of co-option by the West such as to outweigh the risks, even if counted as modest, entailed by sacrificing the support of other Third World states? It would not seem so. What co-option holds out to the oil-rich countries is by and large what they are getting, or are likely to get, in any event. It would be another matter if the major OPEC states were indeed confronted with a choice between co-option into the club of the developed and capitalist states and the threat of serious counter-measures by the West. But that is not their choice today and in all probability will never be their choice. There is no evidence that they have ever taken seriously the prospect that the developed states—or, rather, the United States—might undertake to use force against them, and with good reason. Nor is there much evidence that the oil-rich countries have taken seriously the prospect that the security of their investments in the developed states may one day be threatened, whether as a result of the oil prices they may exact or as a result of their continuing to champion the claims of the Southern states in the manner they have to date. Despite endless warnings against the folly of America's policy of confrontation with OPEC, this country has remained the principal arms supplier to the major OPEC states. And just as it has not denied these states access to the most modern weapons, neither has it denied them access to the technology needed for rapid development. The confrontation the United States is so regularly accused of pursuing against OPEC has been exaggerated beyond any reasonable measure. In reality, what confrontation we have had has been carried on within the framework of a larger under-standing and agreement.*

* Within the framework of this larger understanding and agreement, differences of course persist and the jockeying for position goes on. Thus American policy has sought to limit, if not to break, the OPEC role of leadership of the developing world by pointing to the effects higher oil prices have had on developing economies and by calling attention to the "inadequate" aid OPEC has afforded to the poor states. It may be argued that opposition to this role is the functional equivalent of opposition to—indeed, confrontation with—OPEC, since its abandonment would mean abandonment

The Future of Inequality

In these circumstances, there has been no need for the principal OPEC countries to choose between North and South, a choice that for obvious reasons they will continue to resist for some time to come.* Today, admission to the circle of developed and capitalist states can only be undertaken, if at all, on terms designed by the circle's members. The reality of inequality will therefore persist despite the appearance of equality. Moreover, it is very doubtful that this appearance might compensate for those advantages gained by continuing to play the leadership role on behalf of the oppressed. Eventually, of course, the choice that is resisted today will have to be made. But by the time it must be made, the likelihood is that we shall be witness to the creation of centers of economic and military power that are quite capable of admitting themselves into the charmed circle.

The experience to date with OPEC may nevertheless prove misleading in its implications for the prospects of maintaining Southern solidarity. It may be that this solidarity, never very great in any event, will soon fall apart under the strains introduced by the many and growing differences marking the circumstances and interests of

---

of OPEC. But this is surely to exaggerate the importance of Southern solidarity to OPEC's very survival. In attempting to sow dissension between OPEC and other developing states, American policy has sought to contain OPEC, not to break it by open confrontation. There is every reason to believe that American policymakers have come to fear the consequences of "breaking" OPEC much more than the consequences of preserving it (even while containing its actions). For the breaking of OPEC is seen as ushering in radical regimes in the major, and still conservative, oil producing states. And even apart from this vital consideration, American interests are not found, on balance, to have suffered from higher oil prices. Quite the contrary, these interests are now seen to have been benefitted. Why, then, should the United States seek OPEC's demise, as long as the effects of OPEC's example and role as champion of the South can be limited? Moreover, there is every reason to assume that the prime movers in OPEC—Saudi Arabia and Iran—appreciate American policy. Although refusing to forego the role they have cast themselves in, they are only too careful not to push that role too far.

* Hansen writes. "Given the risks to these countries—especially those located in the Middle East—of opting unambiguously for *either* the 'North' or the 'South,' the most likely goal of most OPEC countries will be to keep both bridges open" ("Political Economy of North-South Relations," p. 943). The gradual *embourgeoisement* of OPEC is seen as the probable result of growing power, though only occurring over a period of time.

the developing countries. Eventually, it seems bound to do so, if only because differential rates of development will be expressed, particularly in the case of the larger states, in aspirations for regional hegemony. A semblance of Southern solidarity may nevertheless survive emerging conflicts for local supremacy. Certainly, the aspirants for such supremacy may be expected to justify their goals in terms of opposition to the "old" order, much as rising and ambitious powers have done in the past. Even so, the appearance of states in the South with clearly hegemonic aspirations would effectively put an end to the post-colonial era and, with it, whatever reality Southern solidarity may possess today.

In the meantime, the promise of an accommodationist strategy that is designed to leave the present order essentially intact will depend not only upon the cohesiveness of the South but upon the cohesiveness of the developed and capitalist states as well. Although it is Southern solidarity that has been generally seen as the critical variable in determining the course of North-South relations in the years ahead, there is a growing suspicion that this emphasis may well be misplaced. An accommodationist strategy presupposes that conflicts of interest among the industrial democracies will be contained and that a basic unity of purpose and action will be preserved. There is no assurance of this basic unity, however. Not that a serious threat to it is likely to arise from what are primarily divergent economic interests internal to the developed economies. Although such conflicts may put the consensus of the developed countries under considerable strain—as they did in the years of the early 1970s—there seems little prospect that in and of themselves these conflicts might lead to a fundamental break and the subsequent attempt by Western Europe and Japan to create largely self-sufficient regional blocs. Unless we are to assume that traditional security concerns are no longer relevant in state relations, these regional blocs would be viable if the developed state(s) forging them proved able and willing to provide not only for its security but for the security of region. There is no evidence today of such willingness on the part of either Western European or Japan to undertake the necessary sacrifices—and risks—to create indepen-

dently viable regional blocs. If anything, there appears less willingness than ever to undertake a course leading to strategic independence from the United States. Speculation may persist over the
prospects of a Euro-Arabia, but it is meaningless as long as Europe is
unable to provide for its own security, let alone for the security of its
putative Middle Eastern partners. Even in Africa, recent events have
strikingly demonstrated the shallowness of regional pretensions
where there is no effective power to give substance to those pretensions when needed. It is not to Western Europe that the African
states have directed their hostile or friendly attention, first over
Angola and subsequently over Rhodesia, but to the United States.

If these considerations are once accepted, however, how might a
serious threat to the cohesiveness of the developed and capitalist
states arise? Those who assume it might yet arise through an American policy of confrontation with the OPEC states have not made and
can scarcely make a persuasive, or even a plausible, case. Even if we
assume a "failure" of American policy toward the Third World as a
whole—that is, continued American resistance to most of the demands embodied in the New International Economic Order—it is
difficult to see the consequences of this failure leading to the breakup
of the present order. No doubt, a replay of American policy in the
1960s, only this time on a still larger scale, would threaten such a
breakup. But the prospects for this appear altogether negligible. The
fear of an American counter-reaction to the rising assertiveness of
the new states, a counter-reaction that would take a military expression, may be set aside.

What appears more plausible is the prospect that there may be a
gradual erosion of American power throughout the world and that the
credibility of such power as does remain will correspondingly decline. A sharply reduced American role might also be expected to
signal a turn toward greater protectionism on the part of this country,
since an increasingly protectionist America would form the logical
economic counterpart of a policy of political-strategic contraction.
Even without a sharp turn toward greater protectionism, the atrophy
of American power would surely remove the principal means of

American leadership among the developed non-Communist states of the North. In these circumstances, Western Europe and, to a lesser extent, Japan would no longer have the incentive to retain the essential solidarity that has heretofore characterized their relations with this country. Indeed, in these circumstances, Western Europe and Japan would be increasingly confronted with the choice of either attempting to establish relatively tightly controlled regional systems in which they would play the dominant political-military and economic roles or of remaining politically and militarily passive while trying to strike the best possible deals with those developing countries on which they will remain dependent for raw materials. The former alternative cannot be excluded. It is extremely unlikely, however, since it assumes an assertion of political will that seems quite at odds with the present character of these societies—certainly of the Western European states and most likely of Japan as well. Instead, the far more likely outcome would be a period of prolonged uncertainty and instability during which the developing countries would press whatever advantages they could while the then-fragmented democratic capitalist societies would perforce yield on many issues that the presence of the United States today saves them—or, in the eyes of many of their apologists, prevents them—from yielding.

It is unnecessary to speculate on the more detailed consequences of this choice that would likely follow a marked erosion of American power. Even if we set aside entirely the role of the Soviet Union in such a world, though it would be critical, it is clear that the character of North-South relations would undergo considerable, perhaps even radical, change. The disjunction between order and power, already apparent in the present international system, would be magnified many-fold. Indeed, that disjunction might be rapidly resolved in favor of the contenders for a new order who have few of the reservations about the maintenance and employment of military power that mark the outlook of the states of Western Europe and Japan. The disutility of military power is not a Southern obsession. It is one thing to reject romantic notions about the power of the poor and desperate among the new states and quite another to dismiss the prospect that the rising and ambitious among these states would refrain from exploiting their growing military power in an increasingly fragmented international system.

These considerations point to the continued significance of American power in preserving the basic unity of the industrial democracies and in shaping the course of North-South relations. It may be argued that in the medium term, at any rate, the likely prospect is that this power will be maintained and, with its maintenance, the solidarity of the developed states assured. If this argument is accepted, we are back to the issue of Southern solidarity and to the prospects held out by a strategy of co-optation through accommodation. It is this strategy, we have earlier noted, that is seen to afford the principal opportunity for blunting the Southern challenge to the existing order. It is through co-optation that the hope is held out not only of breaking a solidarity that, for all its weaknesses, is acknowledged to threaten the present international system but of strengthening this system by giving it a broader measure of consensus.

Is a strategy of co-optation through accommodation feasible and would its consequences prove desirable? A positive response has drawn upon the earlier experience of class accommodation within the Western democracies. "Is the present struggle between the classes of nation-states," Tom J. Farer asks, "not susceptible to mitigation by the employment of an analogous strategy of accommodation?" * He answers by arguing that, on balance, the effort to apply an accommodationist strategy to North-South relations seems no more difficult, and perhaps even easier, than the prior case of class confrontation. The basis for this optimism rests on the belief that with respect to the "political axis of confrontation" the new states are in reality asking for very little. Even over economic issues, the conflict may be readily managed not only because here as well the demands are modest but because those to be co-opted are small in number, less committed

* Farer, "United States and the Third World," p. 92. The analogy between class confrontation and interstate conflict has been drawn by many writers in the past. On the eve of World War II, it was put forth by E. H. Carr as the most useful way of considering the problem of peaceful change in international society. Cf. *The Twenty Years' Crisis, 1919–1939* (London: Macmillan, 1939), pp. 212ff.

to human equality as a general condition than we are, and quite capable of delivering their huge constituencies. It is with the governing elites of a very few states that we must come to terms. Accommodation will be facilitated, Farer concludes, by the "very small number of representatives that have to be co-opted into senior decision-making roles in the management structure of the international economy. In Africa, only Nigeria. In Latin America, Brazil and Venezuela, and perhaps Mexico. In the Middle East, Saudi Arabia and Iran. And in Asia, India and Indonesia." *

The persuasiveness of this analogy cannot be made to turn upon the feasibility, as such, of co-option. No doubt, co-option is, in some sense, feasible. But the relevant issue is the deeper meaning, the more lasting consequences, of co-option. This issue cannot be usefully addressed without acknowledging that there are different kinds of co-option and that the significance of the process depends upon the nature of the system in which it occurs and the differences that separate the would-be co-opters from those to be co-opted. Even if we neglect for the moment the differences separating co-opters from co-opted, we cannot neglect the fact that in the instant case co-option is prescribed for what remains in essence an anarchical system. Within domestic society, the promise of co-option is one of mitigating the struggle for wealth and power. That promise has not always been realized. When it has been, it is not only because of the "reasonableness" of the contending parties but also because the process of co-option has occurred within an order that sets reasonably well-defined and effective limits to social conflict.

It is the absence of such order in the greater society of states that necessarily gives rise to the prospect that co-option, even if successful in the immediate sense, may eventually serve only to increase, rather than to allay, the struggle for wealth and power. At least, this prospect must always prove to be very real unless one assumes the emergence of forces that are capable of setting effective limits to the perennial conflicts of states. In the present period, such limits are

* Farer, "United States and the Third World," p. 93.

commonly found in the interdependencies that characterize the international system. But these interdependencies, we have argued, are themselves as much—if not more—a source of conflict as they are a source of order and constraint. If the more lasting consequences of co-option are made to turn largely on the "reality of national interdependence," * these consequences must raise all of the questions that interdependence raises. Co-option, like interdependence, may only create in the end a greater need for order without providing any assurance this need will be met; it may only serve to exacerbate the struggle for wealth and power rather then mitigate it.

As applied to North-South relations, the difficulties attending a strategy of co-option through accommodation arise in part because international society is not domestic society. It does not follow that the success of such a strategy is precluded in international society, only that it is made more difficult and uncertain. Its difficulty today, moreover, is due not only to the absence of a social framework that provides some stability to the process of accommodation but to the markedly heterogeneous character of the parties involved in this process. This pervasive heterogeneity finds no meaningful parallel to the differences that earlier separated classes within the state. Where class conflict issued in successful accommodation, it was because adversaries ultimately shared the same values. However much one side may have denied these values in practice, in the end this common commitment—even though attended by the threat or actuality of force—provided the balm of compromise. In the international society of today, it would be ludicrous to attempt even the vaguest articulation of those values common to the participants in the struggle over a new distribution of wealth and power. Instead, we are thrown back on the all too ambiguous reality of interdependence and, of course, the presumably common desire to avoid serious international conflict.

---

* They apparently do so for Farer (Ibid., p. 97), who declares: "One of the potential strengths of the present international system is the reality of national interdependence which creates an objective need for cooperation and consequently for accepting sharp restraints on the competitive aspects of interstate relations. The principal danger is an irrational assessment of risks and opportunities."

It is chiefly for these reasons that a strategy of co-option through accommodation must be viewed with a substantial measure of skepticism. It may be argued that despite the hazards of this strategy there appears no viable alternative. Even if true, those hazards ought to be recognized for what they are. No useful purpose is served by viewing co-option as a strategy in which all may gain rather than one in which the gains of some occur only at the expense of others. This view is misleading even as applied to the experience of class confrontation within states. It is particularly misleading as applied to the conflicts between states. Nevertheless, it is given an apparent plausibility in the present context by the penchant for interpreting the challenge to international inequality as primarily a challenge to an economic system. Given favorable prospects for continuing growth in the global product, there seems no apparent reason why changes in that system may not be made to the ultimate gain of all parties. At the deepest level, however, it is not inequalities of wealth but of power that are being challenged; and whereas inequalities of wealth may be altered—and even narrowed—to everyone's gain, the same may not be said of inequalities of power. This is above all the case where the uses to which power will be put are left entirely to the discretion of each power holder.

Will the present beneficiaries of the international system prove able to control the power aspirations of those who will sooner or later seek no more, though no less, than what others have sought before them? Is a strategy of co-option through accommodation at best of little more than marginal relevance here? One may doubt that it is. Co-option can only promise that the disaffected will come to view the international system as do those who presently play a dominant role in the system. But even if that promise were to be realized, it would not preclude the potentially stronger among the disaffected from also aspiring to play an ever increasing role in the system. In order to do so, it will be necessary to achieve the capability of supplying one's own weapons, including eventually nuclear weapons. For those who are able to pursue it, the logic of the challenge to inequality is ultimately the logic of nuclear proliferation. In turn, the logic of nuclear proliferation is one of decreasing control over the international system by those who are its present guardians.

It is banal to conclude that the power structure of the future will evolve in a manner largely independent of our wishes and designs. Yet it is probably no less true for being banal. We can also be reasonably sure that the challenge to the present system will eventually give rise not so much to a new system but to a new hierarchy. That the new hierarchy will prove more benign than those of the past can be little more than a profession of hope in a world that seems destined to repeat the cycle of nation-state development we have already witnessed in the West.

Index

Index

Index

Index

Index

211

Index

decline of, 175; equality of, individual equality and, 61–64, 155; equality of opportunity for, 130–132, 147–150; equality of opportunity and role of, 136; freedom of action of, 58–61, 66, 67, 137, 175; independence of, *see* Independence; interdependence of, *see* Interdependence; international welfare community and, 171, 172*n*; minimal subsistence and, 136; nation equated with, 21; new, *see* New states; new egalitarianism's view of, 58, 61–65, 130–132, 156, 178–179; new political sensibility's view of, 58, 134, 137–138, 151–155; persistence of, 173; public welfare within, vs. welfare of those outside, 110–112, 139–140, 166–168 (*see also* New political sensibility, fellow-citizens and mankind not differentiated in); sacrifice commanded by, 151; self-help right of, *see* Self-help, right of; sovereignty of, *see* Sovereignty; "tamed," 138; welfare, 143–145

State system, 70, 186; development constrained by, 168; inequalities inherent in, 169; new egalitarianism and, 75, 117; self-help principle and, 4–6

Status, inequalities of, 19–20, 106, 107

Status quo, international law and change in, 11–12

Stokes, Eric, 28*n*

Stone, Julius, 14*n*, 68, 124*n*, 140*n*, 172*n*

Subsistence, minimal level of, *see* Minimal subsistence

Suez, Anglo-French intervention at, 41

Sumberg, Theodore A., 56*n*

Systeme mixte, 175

Tariff barriers, 182

Tariff preferences, 183

Tawney, R. H., 105*n*

Technology, 99

Territorial integrity, 180*n*

Terrorism, 91

Theory of Justice, A (Rawls), 139*n*

Third World, *see* New states

Thornton, A. P., 26*n*

Thucydides, 4, 62

Timor, Portuguese, 180*n*

Trade, 15, 32, 101*n*, 163

Treaty, "unequal," 19

Trusteeship, British, 23*n*, 28

Twenty Years' Crisis, The (Carr), 25*n*, 31*n*

Underdeveloped countries, *see* New states

"Unequal treaty," 19

United Nations, 33, 34, 39; sanctions by, against Rhodesia, 81*n*

United Nations Charter, 33–34, 180*n*

United Nations Conference on Trade and Development (UNCTAD), 48

United Nations General Assembly, 39*n*, 59, 66*n*

United States: colonialism and, 40–43; decolonization and, 40–41; growing demand for equality in, 111; OPEC and policy of, 192, 195; power of, 47–48, 195–197; refusal to respond to demands for change, 184–185, 187; as richest country, 85–86

Vattel, E. de, 140*n*

Venezuela, 198

Vernon, Raymond, 176*n*

Vietnam, United States intervention in, 45–48

Voting strength of new states, 72

Vulnerability: of developed states, 76, 84–86, 90–91, 110; interdependence and, 97